California Wine Country

The Most Beautiful Wineries, Vineyards, and Destinations

Randy Leffingwell
Foreword by Francis Ford Coppola
Voyageur Press

Best Wines and Wineries Lists by the Editors of Voyageur Press

Dedication

For Carolyn, with thanks for the many pleasures of your company

Copyright © 2002 by Randy Leffingwell

All rights reserved. No part of this work may be reproduced or used in any form by any means—graphic, electronic, or mechanical, including photocopying, recording, taping, or any information storage and retrieval system—without written permission of the publisher.

Edited by Michael Dregni
Designed by Maria Friedrich
Printed in China

02 03 04 05 06 5 4 3 2 1

Library of Congress Cataloging-in-Publication Data

Leffingwell, Randy, 1948—
  California wine country : the most beautiful wineries, vineyards, and destinations / Randy Leffingwell ; foreword by Francis Ford Coppola.
        p. cm. — (A pictorial discovery guide)
Includes index.
  ISBN 0-89658-491-7
  1. Wine and wine making—California—Guidebooks. 2. Wineries—California—Guidebooks. 3. California—Guidebooks.
I. Title. II. Series.
  TP557 .L445 2002
  641.2'209764—dc21
                                2002002567

Distributed in Canada by Raincoast Books, 9050 Shaughnessy Street, Vancouver, B.C. V6P 6E5

Published by Voyageur Press, Inc.
123 North Second Street, P.O. Box 338
Stillwater, MN 55082 U.S.A.
651-430-2210, fax 651-430-2211
books@voyageurpress.com
www.voyageurpress.com

Educators, fundraisers, premium and gift buyers, publicists, and marketing managers: Looking for creative products and new sales ideas? Voyageur Press books are available at special discounts when purchased in quantities, and special editions can be created to your specifications. For details contact the marketing department at 800-888-9653.

Certain vineyard and wine names and logo designs are the property of trademark holders. We use them for identification purposes only.

The front matter:
Page one:
Grape vines at Gainey Vineyard

Page two:
Old-growth Pinot Noir vines turn brilliant red after the autumn harvest at Madonna Vineyards.

Page three:
Top left:
Chateau Souverain
Middle left:
Niebaum-Coppola Winery
Bottom left:
Jordan Vineyard & Winery
Top right:
Opus One
Middle right:
Greystone
Bottom right:
California wine country farmstead

Page four:
Top:
Cabernet Sauvignon grapes
Middle left:
Autumn's grape harvest
Bottom left:
A tray full of Cabernet Sauvignon grapes
Bottom right:
Collecting full grape trays

Page five:
Top left:
Wrapping towers of grape trays at San Bernabe for freezing and shipment to Bonny Doon Vineyards
Middle left:
Juice-covered hands pressing grapes at Livingston Moffett Winery
Top right:
Winemaker Etienne Cowper siphons a taste from a barrel of port at Mount Palomar Winery.
Bottom:
Harvesting grapes at San Bernabe Vineyards

Page six:
A late-February storm casts a rainbow over vineyards along Napa's Silverado Trail.

Page seven:
Top:
Toasting barrels at Seguin Moreau Tonnellerie
Bottom:
Ancient-redwood aging barrels in the old winery at Buena Vista Carneros from the time of founder Agoston Haraszthy.

Title page:
Inset image:
From left to right: E. & J. Gallo Twin Valley California Sauvignon Blanc; Niebaum-Coppola 1999 Rutherford Zinfandel; Wild Horse 1999 ENZ Vineyard Lime Kiln Valley Sauvignon Blanc; Shenandoah 1998 Daphne Late Harvest Sauvignon Blanc; Tobin James 2000 Paso Robles Charisma dessert wine; Jordan 1997 Sonoma County Cabernet Sauvignon; J. Filippi Ruby Port; Sierra Vista 1997 El Dorado, 5-Star Reserve Syrah; Gainey 2000 Santa Ynez Valley Riesling; Bernardus 1996 Bien Nacido Vineyard Pinot Noir

Contents

Foreword

For almost thirty years, my family and I have had the privilege of growing grapes, making wine, and living in beautiful Napa Valley. We look forward to the first hint of green that signals bud break and rejoice as the flowering mustard paints the vineyards neon yellow. The rumble of tractors is part of the change of our seasons, and the heady smell of fermenting grapes represents the culmination of a year of work.

From north to south, California wine country is an enchanted place. Wine evokes passion among those who practice the art and pleasure for those who partake in it. Randy Leffingwell's book captures the beauty that lies down so many country lanes.

California wine country has attracted people from diverse backgrounds with one thing in common: a passion for this delicious and sensuous beverage. Wine was always part of my life growing up. The wine most often on our table was not Italian, but from California, and when my grandfather and uncles practiced a little home winemaking it was with grapes purchased from California and shipped by rail to New York.

I first fell in love with the wine country in the early 1970s, as the wine boom was just starting. We were on our way back to California after filming *The Rain People* across the country. My associate—and now dear friend—George Lucas was from Modesto, and our plan was to drive back through northern California and on down to his home. I don't know what I expected when we arrived in St. Helena in the Napa Valley. I thought I would find a very European village with little chalets, but instead it was a charming, but sleepy farming town. The country-side was beautiful and peaceful and very appealing to me. It was not too many years later that we finally purchased part of what had been the famed Inglenook Estate and started our own winemaking odyssey.

This book takes you on a wonderful armchair tour of California wine country—a tour from past to present, as well as through the many diverse growing regions. And once you've finished your armchair travels, buy a ticket and come see us for yourself. The land, the wine, and the people are waiting to welcome you.

Francis Ford Coppola

Chapter One

Vines and Wines

The History of
California Wine Country

O rganized religion in America has been both friend and foe to wine. The colonists who landed at Jamestown, Virginia—many of whom were fleeing church persecution—made use of native wild grapes to create their own wine as early as 1609. Farther north, the Pilgrims at Plymouth, Massachusetts, celebrated in 1623 their third anniversary in the New World by serving their first Thanksgiving feast accompanied by their own wine.

To encourage agriculture and industry in the New World, the colonial government promoted planting vines and fermenting wines. While the Pilgrims celebrated Thanksgiving, the Virginia Colonial Assembly enacted a law in 1623 requiring each home to plant ten new vines. The wine made from these vines was awful by all accounts. Nevertheless, Virginia soon organized contests to determine the best of its local wines. Judges, however, could declare no winners.

No matter to the Colonials. Seeking escape from the rigors of life, they had already discovered fermented apple cider, distilled whiskey, and rum, all of which were inexpensive to produce and numbingly effective. The Commonwealth of Massachusetts not only branded the scarlet letter "A" on the chests of adulterers but also sewed a large letter "D" on others proclaiming their crime as drunkenness, usually on "demon" rum.

On North America's Pacific Coast, the Spanish Franciscan missionaries, who first accompanied the conquistadores in their conquest of Mexico in the early 1500s, brought sacramental wine with them as they started north from Baja in 1769. The conquistadores and accompanying padres traveled from Mexico's western peninsula to establish Spanish outposts in what they termed Alta California to discourage English and Russian trappers and hunters from settling in Spanish territory. These Spanish missions also set out to "civilize" the natives and convert them to Christianity; in the process, they introduced them to, among other things, wine.

The Cross, the Sword, and the Vine

In 1769, the first Spanish expeditions left Baja to settle Alta California. The party of the newly appointed governor of Alta California, Don Gaspár de Portolá, also included padre Junípero Serra, who had led the Franciscans in Baja California and was now assigned to supervise the establishment of missions in the new territory. Their trek was grueling, and the expedition spent four and a half months walking the 1,000 miles from Loretto Mission in far southern Baja to reach San Diego.

Supplies for Serra's missions and the soldier garrisons that accompanied them were sent by ship, but even the sea voyage was harried. One ship disappeared. Scurvy, caused by poor nutrition from lack of fresh fruits and vegetables, killed nearly all the crew of two more ships. But supplies finally arrived at Serra's first mission, San Diego de Alcalá, including wine with which the padre administered the sacraments to his new Indian converts.

Beginning in 1778 and 1779, the supply convoys from Mexico ceased arriving with their accustomed regularity, a sign of the impending downfall of the Spanish colonial rule. Without their supply of sacramental wine, the missions had to cancel daily masses. The padres had long proved their resourcefulness in surviving in Alta California, and they now did so again by planting grape vines. Father Pablo de Mugartegui was the first to plant vines, in late 1778, at Mission San Juan Capistrano, California's second mission, and the

MISSION SAN DIEGO DE ALCALA, CALIFORNIA, FOUNDED 1769

Mission San Diego de Alcalá postcard, 1930s
Spanish padre Junípero Serra began construction of the first mission in Alta California—Mission San Diego de Alcalá—in 1769. Eventually, twenty-one missions would be built, stretching all the way to Sonoma.

Mission San Francisco de Solano

The northernmost of the Spanish missions in Alta California, San Francisco de Solano, was planned in 1821 and begun in 1823 as a Spanish effort to stop Russian settlement in its territory. Spanish soldiers, padres, and Miwok natives completed construction of the mission in early spring 1824, dedicating the church on April 4. That same year, the padres were cultivating grape vines with plans to make communion wine.

General Mariano Vallejo

In 1833, General Mariano Vallejo was assigned to govern Spain's California territories. Vallejo was rewarded with an enormous rancho in Petaluma, where he began growing vines to make wine. He was pictured here with several of his daughters and granddaughters.

first mission wines were made in 1781 and 1782. As further missions were established all the way north to Mission San Francisco de Asis on San Francisco Bay, later friars also planted grapes. By 1824, the padres were cultivating vines at their northernmost outpost, Mission San Francisco de Solano at Sonoma.

The role of the California missions in the beginning of California winemaking was fundamental, but their final entry in the history was anticlimactic, if not tragic. Severely strapped for funds, the Spanish and Mexican governments decided to secularize the missions and troop garrisons. Beginning in 1833, Spanish rulers assigned General Mariano Guadalupe Vallejo to govern the territories through this secularization process, and these huge compounds were released from government and church authority and financial support. Many padres resented this upheaval and abandonment: As they left their homes, some fathers damaged the missions they had built and destroyed their carefully cultivated vines.

This mattered little to the Spanish government. For successfully divesting Spain of expensive obligations, the Spanish rulers rewarded Vallejo with an enormous rancho in Petaluma, northwest of the San Francisco Bay. Vallejo bestowed other grants on those who helped him, including a grant in 1836 to transplanted Missouri frontiersman George Calvert Yount, who had repaired Vallejo's rancho and garrisons. For these simple labors, Vallejo gave Yount an 11,800-acre parcel called Rancho Caymus, containing nearly the entire Napa Valley.

By 1838, Yount had begun planting his valley with Criolla Mission grapes from Sonoma Mission cuttings. By the end of the 1840s, other farmers had established vineyards around Napa and Sonoma, west to Sacramento and south around San Francisco Bay through Santa Clara, Alameda, and Contra Costa Counties.

Pioneers of the California Wine Industry

On January 28, 1848, a carpenter named Jim Marshall discovered gold at Johan Sutter's sawmill site fifty miles up the American River from Sacramento. By June, 2,000 men were digging in the riverbed, and the Gold Rush was on. Yet for every gold digger who succeeded, hundreds failed. Many soon learned that California offered other opportunities. Massachusetts farmer J. W. Osborne had forsaken the gold hunt and by 1855, had a sixty-acre vineyard growing near Napa, the largest at the time. Among his other accomplishments, Osborne successfully introduced *Vitis vinifera* Zinfandel and Muscat of Alexandria grapes to northern California.

To promote vine planting, the newly formed California State Legislature exempted vineyards from taxes for four years beginning in 1859. The strategy worked. While some failed gold prospectors already had planted vines, many more vineyards opened in El Dorado County, not far from Sutter's sawmill site, and nearly sixty wineries covered the Sonoma Valley floor with "a blanket of vines," as one chronicler wrote. From 1858 to 1860, the number of vineyard acres doubled; 300 acres were now planted with some 190,000 vines throughout Placer, Tuolumne, Amador, Nevada, Calaveras, and El Dorado Counties in Gold Country alone.

In the early 1860s, the pioneering legends of California winemaking founded their legacies. German settler Charles Krug established a winery in Napa Valley in 1861, and fifteen years later he was producing 500,000 gallons annually. Another German, Jacob Schram, bought hillside land near Calistoga in the upper Napa Valley, and his vineyards and winery became legends for the next half-century. Others also pioneered vineyards, including Antoine Delmas, Charles Lefranc, and Pierre Pellier in Santa Clara and Jacob Nath in the Sierra foothills.

By the early 1870s, Hamilton W. Crabb was producing wines from his 360-acre Napa Valley vineyard in Oakville, planted with the best *vinifera* varieties available. He built his winery from native stone and, aiming for the highest quality possible, named it To-Kalon, ancient Greek for "The Highest Good." To-Kalon became the valley's largest winery by 1880, with countless experimental varieties grown in pursuit of Crabb's lofty goal. (In 1899, Crabb's family lost the vineyard. The University of California acquired twenty acres of To-Kalon in 1906 that it still uses as an experimental vineyard. The original winery burned in mid 1939 and languished until Robert Mondavi acquired To-Kalon in 1965. Striving for his own "highest good," Mondavi planted his vines and built his own Spanish Mission–style winery there.)

The German Beringer brothers—winemaker Jacob and businessman Frederick—made their first wines starting in 1876. They eventually built a stunning stone Victorian home and winery in St. Helena in the upper Napa Valley.

San Francisco banker William Watson started a 1,000-acre vineyard and winery in Rutherford that he named Inglenook. In 1879, Watson sold it to a wine-loving Finnish sea captain named Gustave Niebaum who had accumulated his fortune transporting Alaskan furs. Niebaum took his commitment seriously. He returned to Europe, took winemaking classes, and came back to

Agoston Haraszthy de Mokesa
Grape grower and winemaker Agoston Haraszthy established his Buena Vista kingdom in Sonoma in 1856. In 1861, he returned from Europe with more than 100,000 vine cuttings representing some 1,400 grape varieties from Spain, France, Italy, and Germany; these vines bore grapes at many California wineries over the next several decades—and may have introduced the parasitic Phylloxera root louse to the state.

Inglenook to plant selected French and German regional varieties. He was the first in Napa Valley confident enough of his product to bottle his wines under his own label.

While Niebaum completed his fifth and sixth harvests, two young businessmen, William Bourne and Everett Wise, set out to aid, expand, and control the wine business. They built a three-story monument to their boldness in St. Helena that they called Greystone. When hundreds of Chinese stonemasons and carpenters finished the building in 1889, it was the largest stone winery in the world. Its magnificence fit Bourne and Wise's ambitions perfectly: to assist winemakers in getting the best price for their products.

Most of the hundred or so winemakers in Napa and Sonoma Counties in the 1880s were small operations with limited capital and little storage space for aging new wine properly. The two young entrepreneurs were their own bankers, and they certainly had the space to age wine within Greystone's walls. Bourne's riches came from his Empire Gold Mine that had yielded its young owner more than $10 million by the 1880s. They advanced winemakers ten cents a gallon on wine stored at Greystone. They also undertook to make wine from the freshly pressed juice that customers brought in. Bourne and Wise established a cooperage to make barrels within Greystone's yards.

Across the Mayacamas Mountains that separate Sonoma from Napa, a grape grower and winemaker named Agoston Haraszthy de Mokesa had established his own kingdom. Haraszthy was a legend in his own mind long before he became one in California. He claimed he was a count and a colonel, though he was neither. Born in Hungary, he immigrated to Wisconsin in 1842, reached California in 1848, became the sheriff of San Diego, and finally arrived in Sonoma in 1856. He bought a vineyard from General Vallejo's brother and named it Buena Vista for its beautiful views. His early efforts at winemaking won him awards and medals at local fairs. Instead of growing grapes on bottomland next to water, Haraszthy planted on hillsides, proving the California climate was sufficiently moist to grow without irrigating. He also used cheap redwood casks for aging instead of expensive oak; redwood casks would become the main aging method in California for the next century. In 1858, he wrote the state's first guide to California wine-grape growing.

Haraszthy's greatest contribution to California winemaking was his trip to Europe in 1861 to examine contemporary vineyard practices and winemaking techniques. Travelling under the auspices of the state governor's office, he returned with more than 100,000 vine cuttings representing about 1,400 different varieties from Spain, France, Italy, and Germany. Sadly, he was no record-keeper: He identified all of these cuttings under only 500 names. Over time, his sons Arpad and Attila propagated these vines and sold cuttings to growers throughout the state without properly identifying them, leading to confusion that exists even today.

Haraszthy continually expanded Buena Vista, but by 1866, he was financially overextended. He asked the state legislature to reimburse him for his European trip and his vines, but that was not part of the governor's agreement, and the legislature refused. Haraszthy left California bound for Nicaragua to establish a sugar cane plantation. Arpad and Attila both married daughters of General Vallejo and attempted to continue their father's winemaking legacy. But Buena Vista fell on hard times in the 1870s, when the Phylloxera root louse began destroying the Haraszthy vineyards as well as others throughout California. The parasitic insect had likely been imported from Europe on the very vines Haraszthy had brought back.

Finding Gold in Southern California Grapes

Through the late 1800s, Sonoma's valley floor, the "blanket of vines," produced about 40 percent of all California wine. The second-largest winemaking region was Los Angeles County. A Frenchman, appropriately named Jean-Louis Vignes—his last name being French for "vines"—was the first to establish a vineyard in Los Angeles: In 1833, he began growing grapes alongside the Los Angeles River on land just across today's Hollywood Freeway, Highway 101, from the downtown Union Railway Station. Contemporary observers J. Wagner and J. B. Hayes wrote in their 1876 *Historical Sketches of Los Angeles County* that San Francisco buyers paid Vignes and others as much as 12½¢ a pound or $250 per ton for Los Angeles grapes in 1849; within a decade, Los Angeles growers shipped more than forty tons to Bay-area producers. While Los Angeles may have seemed an inauspicious site for a vineyard—too hot, dusty, and sunny—most of Vignes's products were fortified wines, with other alcohol such as brandy added to raise the alcohol content to between 14 and 24 percent. In these early fortified wines, flavor mattered less than the numbing effect.

Another immigration effort lured dozens of ambitious German families from San Francisco to Southern California. These former tradespeople had settled in the Bay area after failing to find fortunes in the riverbeds. The Austrian-born deputy surveyor of Los Angeles County, George Hansen, knew of productive land south of the young city. With Charles Kohler and John Frohling, two ambitious Bay-area German musicians and wine distributors, Hansen created the Los Angeles Vineyards Society in 1857. Hansen had supervised the planting in Los Angeles of 400,000 Mission grape cuttings, mostly from Vignes's competitor, William Wolfskill. In 1859, the first Germans moved onto their twenty-acre vineyard homesteads in their "home along the Santa Ana River," Anaheim—*heim* being German for "home."

In 1860, the German growers made 2,000 gallons of wine. A decade later, Anaheim boasted fifty wineries. In 1880, production reached 1,250,000 gallons when the town claimed 10,000 acres had been planted in grapes for wine, raisins, and table use.

All Southern California wine-grape growing came to a halt beginning in 1883 due to a mysterious disease. Vine leaves and fruit withered; half of Anaheim's vines failed within two years. No one knew the cause. The U.S. Department of Agriculture (USDA) sent one investigator after another to inspect the flying-insect-borne bacterial infections. Finally in 1891, the USDA's Newton Pierce concluded it was an unknown disease, and worse, no cure existed. For his work, the USDA and the winemaking world came to know his name: The plague was christened Pierce's disease. Sensing disaster, the German settlers already had planted oranges or begun brewing beer, and by year end, Anaheim had just fourteen acres of healthy vines.

While Pierce's disease also put Jean-Louis Vignes out

of the wine-grape business and led William Wolfskill into oranges, still other vineyards and wineries continued east of Los Angeles. Huge operations began in the early 1850s in the San Gabriel Valley, founded with cuttings from Mission San Gabriel. Vineyards stretched from Pasadena east and covered hundreds of acres with thousands of vines. Pasadena's Lake Vineyard owner Benjamin Wilson innovated California's first sparkling wine, but even Wilson turned to orange growing when his vineyards died of Pierce's disease.

In the near-desert region around San Bernardino, Secondo Guasti's 5,000-acre Italian Vineyard Company in Cucamonga and other area winemakers survived Pierce's and the Phylloxera louse as the hot climate and sandy soil defeated the disease and pests.

Prospectors who failed to find riches in the rivers instead found gold in the agricultural potential of California's central valleys, where the year-round flow of water from the Merced and San Joaquin Rivers fed the soil. Resettled Easterners and Midwesterners began farming along the San Joaquin in the 1850s and 1860s. But with the arrival of the Transcontinental Railroad in

To-Kalon Vineyard
Robert Mondavi owns the stunning and historically significant To-Kalon Vineyard near St. Helena in Napa County. Mondavi remains one of California's most history-conscious producers.

1869 and the creation of the town of Fresno in 1872, the Golden Valley produced new wealth from experimental irrigated farms. In 1873, a Swedish businessman living in San Francisco, Francis Eisen, slowly bought Central Valley land and planted grapes, gradually expanding to 400 acres by 1888 and producing 300,000 gallons of wine annually. Former mine engineer Robert Barton produced 500,000 gallons from his 700-acre vineyard and winery, which he then sold in 1887 for $1 million.

The hot Central Valley sun was ideal for producing sweet wine even though vintners tried to defy nature by making dry wines as well. But the industry was learning. California was not Europe. Various regions might have coastal fog, but most days that cooling cloud cover burned off. The Golden State got far more sun than French vineyards received. Growers had begun paying closer attention to choosing carefully the grape varieties they raised in certain soils under the advantageous climates. This was the essence of a concept the French call *terroir*, and a sense of California *terroir* was developing among the best and brightest winemakers.

Top:

Niebaum-Coppola Winery

In 1879, Finnish sea captain Gustave Niebaum took over the Inglenook Winery in Rutherford started by banker William Watson. Niebaum's magnificent chateau was 220 feet long and 72 feet wide and required six years to build under the guiding hands of architect William Mooser and winery designer Hamden W. McIntyre. It is now the headquarters of filmmaker Francis Ford Coppola's Niebaum-Coppola Winery.

Right:

Greystone Wine Cellar postcard, 1920s

1301 Greystone Wine Cellar, St. Helena, California.

Funded by more than $10 million in gold-mine earnings, William Bourne and Everett Wise aimed to aid, expand, and control the California wine business from their Greystone mansion in St. Helena. When hundreds of Chinese workers finished the building in 1889, it was the largest stone winery in the world, with vast wine storage areas and its own cooperage.

Fighting to Build a Reputation

While vineyards in Southern California succumbed to Pierce's disease, those in the north were failing under the Phylloxera scourge that had ravaged Europe's grape growers starting in 1867. The grape-crop failures and wine shortages that Phylloxera caused in Europe aided California wines in being introduced to Europeans.

But California's wine reputation was not great. When the wines reached Europe, many were undrinkable. Fearful of the competition, Eastern U.S. grape growers, winemakers, and distributors let California juice spoil on slow trains across the Southwest deserts; others watered down barrels to increase the quantities and improve their profits. A San Francisco research chemist also devised a system of concentrating unfermented grape juice by removing the water, sealing it in barrels, and shipping the dense liquid to Europe and England, where importers added water, started fermentation, and sold finished wine several months later. Fewer heavy barrels were not as bulky as numerous casks of finished wine and so cost less to ship. And because the juice was unfermented, it avoided alcohol taxes. Wine distribution was a business of scoundrels and profit-takers, and the California winemakers were the losers.

Harvesting California grapes, 1900s

While French wine drinkers turned up their noses at California wines, French winemakers were interested in the state's grape *vines*. When French vineyards died in the early 1880s of Phylloxera infestations, French growers bought Californian *Vitis lambrusca* and replanted, grafting native French buds onto imported American roots.

The French turned up their noses at California wine—but French winemakers were interested in the California grape *vines*. America's native *Vitis lambrusca* vines had proven resistant to Phylloxera, and when French vineyards died in the early 1880s of root louse infestations, French growers bought American rootstock and re-planted, grafting native French buds onto imported American roots.

California Wine Becomes Big Business

California's winemaking industry suffered a financial collapse in 1876. Over the preceding years, the state's 139 wineries had harvested too many grapes and pro-duced too much wine for their markets. Hundreds of acres went unpicked; more than half the winemakers quit.

Now, in the 1890s, Pierce's disease and Phylloxera proved to be the industry's second great shakeout, shifting two-thirds of the business from Southern California to the north. Unbeknownst to anyone, the northern vine-yards would be hit by Phylloxera later.

The fortunes of grape growers rose and fell throughout the 1880s and 1890s. Problems stemmed from unsuccessful marketing and inconsistent prod-uct quality. Too many individual voices couldn't present their cause or protect their products all the way to New York or London. In an effort to correct this, seven of the largest merchants—including Charles Kohler, John Frohling, and Arpad Haraszthy—founded the California Wine Association (CWA) in San Fran-cisco in 1894. Within a decade, CWA managed two-thirds of the state's entire output—30 million of the total 44 million gallons from fifty wineries. Each of the CWA wineries sent its grapes or juice to the association's 12-million-gallon Winehaven facility in Richmond, near San Francisco. CWA stored, aged, blended, bottled, and shipped California wine. Its goal was a reliable, predict-able product: When customers anywhere in the world opened a "Calwa" wine, they would know what to expect.

CWA and its short-lived rival, the California Wine Makers Corporation, provided financial security to growers and makers, allowing small farmers to raise the grapes and make the wine that worked best for their vineyard without having to broaden their product line in order to remain in business. For the small winemaker, it was an early acknowledgment that not all grapes grow well in all environments.

There was a downside, however. Most of the CWA's output was labeled Calwa Brand Wine, and sold at four, six, or eight dollars a case for red, white, or "dessert" wines, respectively. But the CWA became powerful, holding almost monopolistic control over the California wine industry. If one contributor failed or quit, the CWA simply blended others in to match the uniform Calwa taste. And as much of the CWA wine was listed only as "Calwa," it took individual makers years to establish their own reputations.

The CWA thrived and reach its zenith after 1914 when the Panama Canal opened, offering a shipping route to markets. During the 1915 Panama-Pa-cific International Exposition in San Francisco, its power and products were on display to a huge audience. Notably lacking, however, were European guests who already were preoccupied with a war beginning back home. It was a de-cades-long battle for drinkers' souls that would doom the CWA.

Railroad gondolas full of wine grapes, 1910s
California winemaking became big business when seven of the largest merchants founded the California Wine Association (CWA) in 1894. By 1900, CWA made 30 million gallons of its Calwa wine annually.

Prohibition: The Fatal Law

In the late 1800s, organized religion—which had introduced wine and vines to the United States—turned around its views on the consumption of wine and other alcohol. Americans could buy whiskey for thirty cents a gallon in 1860, and statistics stated that every man, woman, and child consumed seven and a half gallons per year; logic assures that while most didn't, the few made up for the many. The United States was largely founded by Protestants escaping religious persecution for their beliefs, and while nineteenth-century Protestants drank, they advocated moderation and moral responsibility. This ethic compelled numerous religious groups to adopt the Christian attitude of caring for their fellow man. Temperance groups demanded legislated protection from the evils of alcohol, arguing that for the good of all, the few must be saved from temptation.

Grape crate label, 1930s
The wine industry crashed during the years of Prohibition, and many vineyards turned to producing fruit and table grapes.

The State of Maine outlawed the sale of "spirits" in 1851, and twelve states and territories from Rhode Island to Nebraska joined Maine's example by 1855. Still, as laws passed, consumption increased. Some laws seemed crafted to encourage failure, granting allowances for alcoholic beverages that were grown, fermented, or distilled at people's homes, or allowing for home-consumed alcohol, so long as it was produced in another state.

The Women's Christian Temperance Union arose in the mid 1870s to lead the war for nationally enforced abstinence. By 1895, the union was aided by its strongest and most patient ally, the Anti-Saloon League. It took another twenty years of dedicated work to get the "Drys" in control of Congress, but by the time the House and Senate broke for Christmas recess in 1917, they had sent to the states for ratification temperance legislation in the form of the Constitution's Eighteenth Amendment.

Winemakers pleaded for exemption from Prohibition. They argued their product was not liquor; some even said that wine was a temperate beverage aiding digestion of meals. Yet in selling the public what it wanted—a sweet,

24 percent alcohol drink—the industry was its own worst enemy and gave the Anti-Saloon Leaguers ammunition. Winemakers didn't reckon on the unyielding hardliners who pointed to the thousands of post–World War I depression "winos" littering city streets, incapacitated by California and New York wines. Beer brewers also fought for leniency; they too were disappointed.

On January 16, 1920, the Volstead National Prohibition Act became law. Named after the U.S. representative who introduced it, Andrew J. Volstead, the law provided communal imposition of external control. It achieved none of its hoped-for effects.

The Volstead Act prohibited anything with more than ½ percent of alcohol by volume. Naively, the temperates—God-fearing and law-abiding all—thought they had won; they believed the nation would fall into line. Instead, the nation fell into crime.

Under Prohibition, fundamental rules of economics merely evolved. Demand did not dry up, as the Drys had expected. The Volstead Act just reorganized the suppliers and the supply. Bootleggers and organized crime began supplying alcohol to average citizens who would normally never have considered breaking a law.

The bootleggers focused their attention on distilled spirits as they were easier to produce and enormously more profitable than wine ever could be. The wine business, meanwhile, essentially went out of business. Of course some wineries—including Concannon in Livermore Valley and Beaulieu in Rutherford—continued wine production throughout Prohibition, selling unbottled wine out the back door. But whereas U.S. wineries produced 55 million gallons in 1919, the few remaining wineries made just 3.6 million gallons in 1925, selling finished wine to religious organizations and unfermented juice for home use.

"Home use" was a big loophole. Section 29 of the Volstead Act allowed private individuals to make up to 200 gallons a year or about 1,000 cases of "non-intoxicating cider and fruit juices" for consumption in their own homes. So, many wineries made wine bricks, packaging dried, compressed grape must with yeast blocks and wrapping it up with the stern warning not to mix them, to "not allow illegal fermentation" to take place.

There were other loopholes as well. Sacramental wine was permitted, as neither Volstead nor the Drys dared take on the organized religion that had supported them. The Jewish faith also utilized wine, and several historians recount a wonderful revival of religious faith during the 1920s. Anyone calling himself a rabbi could get a permit to buy wine legally so long as he presented a list of his congregation. Some "overnight rabbis" quickly listed their neighbors, who often had no idea they were members of any organized faith. Finally, the act permitted Americans to consume or sell wine for medicinal purpose, and Paul Masson wasted little time before introducing a "medicinal champagne."

In California, wine brick and unfermented juice sales were so strong that, at first, growers planted more vines. While wine production plummeted, state vineyard acreage increased from 300,000 in 1919 to nearly 600,000 in 1926. Then, history repeated itself: The market crashed from oversupply. Those who couldn't afford to pull out their vines and plant plums or other fruit watched their vineyards grow wild with weeds.

It took another constitutional amendment, the Twenty-First, to end Prohibition, but that hardly erased its effects. The Volstead Act died on December 5, 1933, at the peak of the Great Depression. Americans could barely afford beans let alone an $8 case of Calwa wine. A few grape growers, who had gotten along by raising raisins and table grapes as well as providing fruit for sacramental or medicinal wines and home juices, returned to their old products. The rest tried to raise anything that would sell—to anyone.

Overcoming History

"Plant grapes," a young Julio Gallo advised his friend Homer Clark when he stopped by for a visit one day in late 1931. Clark had sold grapes to Gallo's father, Joseph, and had done custom harvesting for the family during the early days. "In two years," Julio said, "Prohibition is going to be over, and I'm going to need all I can get."

A year later, Joseph Gallo, proud patriarch of a struggling table-grape-growing family business, was dead of self-inflicted gunshot wounds. Brothers Julio and Ernest looked at what was left and shrewdly switched their family business to winemaking. They petitioned the state for permission to hold their grapes' juice—Prohibition-speak for "wine"—until it was again legal to sell it for purposes beyond religion and health. Other perceptive and far-seeing winemakers followed suit, and even though Prohibition was still the law of the land, they were allowed to make commercial wine with a government permit. In Napa, Beaulieu began quietly increasing production in 1930, and by 1934, it had a large stock of better wine available. Louis Martini and Inglenook also moved quickly back into winemaking.

Yet while there were still more than 400,000 acres of vines in California, after Prohibition was repealed there were fewer than 300 acres of Cabernet, 600 acres each of Pinot Noir and Zinfandel, and only 800 acres of Chardonnay grapes that were salvageable. Many thousands of acres produced sweet grapes for inexpensive wines. The rest of the vineyards were overgrown. Equipment was broken or had been cannibalized or modified to work with apples, plums, avocados, oranges, and other fruits. Fermenting casks and aging barrels had fallen apart or, in the depths of the depression, had been burned on frigid nights to keep other crops from freezing. Those workers who had pruned vines, harvested grapes, operated presses, filled bottles, packed cases, and loaded trucks had gone off to find other work. Prohibition had destroyed the infrastructure of winemaking. Worse, winemakers faced a steep uphill challenge: Older Americans had forgotten what good wine could be. Their children had never learned.

Fortified sweet wines were the favored drink of the Americans who actually drank wine. After Prohibition, three bottles of sweet wine sold for every one bottle of dry. The fortifieds were also less expensive—so much so that during the depression, wine was a cheaper, better-tasting way to get drunk than whiskey. Few individuals would pay more for lower-alcohol dry wines than for high-alcohol sweet fortifieds: It was a legacy that would take thirty-five years to reverse. Even as late as 1953, American winemakers produced 82 million gallons of dessert wine but only 19 million of red and just 9 million of dry white.

Nearly 800 wineries reopened in California in 1934; by 1938, just 212 remained. Many had formed cooperatives to pool limited resources or found

Italian Swiss Colony vineyard postcard, 1950s
The Italian Swiss Colony in Asti was established in 1881 by Italian and Swiss immigrants. By the 1950s, the winery was selling its Italian-style wines with a blend of Disney-like kitsch and tourist appeal.

willing customers among bulk producers such as Gallo and others in the Central Valley. These arrangements kept many winemakers and vineyards in business that otherwise would have failed.

The survivors started rethinking and replanting. Cabernet Sauvignon had weathered Prohibition only at Inglenook, Beaulieu, and a couple other small vineyards. By 1940, more Cabernet as well as Zinfandel and Petite Sirah grapes had been planted.

The practice of labeling grape varieties and regions on the bottles began in the late 1930s. Among the first were Inglenook, Paul Masson at Saratoga southwest of Santa Cruz, Wente in Livermore Valley, Fountain Grove Winery in Santa Rosa, Louis Martini, and Korbell.

Other newcomers set up shop in Napa Valley. Cesare Mondavi moved to the valley from Lodi with his two sons, Robert and Peter, acquiring Sunny St. Helena Winery and later Charles Krug. The Christian Brothers moved into Napa Valley in 1932 to open a new novitiate. They had been crushing grapes and making wine in Martinez since 1882, selling their excess throughout California. The brothers did well until nearly failing under Prohibition. After repeal, an aggressive marketing program under their brand name Mont La Salle made them a nationwide success—so much so that in 1950, the monks bought the huge Greystone Winery.

"Be Considerate—Serve Wine" advertisement, 1950s
The California Wine Advisory Board worked hard to move America's taste to wine with magazine ads such as this featuring artist Norman Rockwell and tips for becoming a wine expert.

The struggling wineries also received expert help in their craft. In 1936, biochemist Maynard Amerine joined the faculty at University of California at Davis, where he remained for thirty-six years, turning the agriculture of grape growing into true science. In 1938, Russian-born, French-trained André Tchelitscheff went to work for George de Latour's Beaulieu. Together, Tchelitscheff and de Latour made winemaking a true art. De Latour already produced a Private Reserve that was aged two years in oak and two more in the bottle. Tchelitscheff stressed the importance of temperature control during fermentation and understood the role of secondary fermentation, the malolactic process during which the fruit's inherent tart acid is converted into softer, syrupy lactic acid. Tchelitscheff would stay at Beaulieu until 1973, but he remained in California advising hundreds of winemakers and grape growers on how to start, create, or improve their techniques and products.

The Importance of Individuals, the Influence of Corporations

World War II was an unexpected boon to California winemaking. During the war years, European wine was not available to American consumers and Eastern wineries clung on to production of sweet dessert wines; these factors opened the market for California wine. GIs returning to the United States after the war had tasted French and other European dry wines; now they sought dry wine, gradually bringing change to America's wine tastes.

Names were gaining public recognition: Tchelitscheff and de LaTour at Beaulieu, Amerine at U. C. Davis, Mondavi at Krug, Martin Ray at Paul Masson,

J. Leland Stewart at Souverain, Fred and Eleanor McCrea at Stony Hill, James Zellerbach at Hanzell in Sonoma, and others. Each of these individuals made choices and decisions. The combined effect was to begin slowly turning around the iceberg that was American taste. It was a formidable task.

These individuals were clearly doing something right, making not only a desirable product but also a respectable profit. In 1943, Canadian whiskey manufacturer, importer, and distributor Joseph E. Seagram bought Paul Masson, seeing in higher-quality California wines a new profit resource. This marked the first corporate attention to wine in the United States. A quarter-century later, liquor conglomerate Heublein acquired Beaulieu in 1969 and, as time went on, also added Inglenook and Christian Brothers. Seagram snared other winemakers before and after Heublein's arrival in the industry, altering in some respects the nature and culture of grape growing and winemaking. Corporate business types arrived fresh from MBA training that taught them the costs of everything but the value of nothing. Some of these new big-business winemakers questioned using $900-per-ton Chardonnay grapes when Thompson seedless grapes could be had for $50. But well-paid corporate winemakers held firm, and even though costs remained high, wine quality, sales, and corporate profits improved.

If corporate acquisitions threatened California winemaking, tourism and Napa and Sonoma's proximity to San Francisco posed two new, unanticipated threats. One legacy of postwar affluence was the creation of the vacation. Before the war, only the wealthy traveled, going far and staying for long periods. Now, with automobiles affordable and jobs plentiful, all Americans could vacation. Rows of lush vines proved to be a destination that attracted visitors, who then needed places to stay and eat.

The same automobiles and good jobs began congesting San Francisco with its growing business population crowded onto the tiny Golden Gate peninsulas. Workers looked longingly at rural family values achievable at the cost of a longer commute from the farming counties. Dedicated farmer-winemakers established the Agricultural Preserve, and by 1968, Napa and Sonoma's soil was safe from suburban development. Tourists, of course, would eventually prove beneficial, bringing cash and taking home cases of local wines. It was a lesson not missed by other regions looking at adapting agricultural lands to tourism.

Then came federal agricultural tax breaks. These lured many individuals into grape growing and winemaking who knew even less than the corporate bean counters. With promises of 150 percent income returns and tax credits for "farming," most of these people understood neither climate nor soil and planted the wrong grapes in the wrong places. Many newcomers learned the one absolute farming truth: The way to end up with a million dollars in farming is to start with five million.

At the appetizer hour, try serving Sherry wine... Nutlike in flavor, mellow amber Sherry is an age-old and perfect invitation to a good dinner. Set out your Sherry alone or with appetizers . . . in cocktail-size portions

The table wines are light and "dry" (not sweet), made especially to accompany main-course dishes. Good table wines to try are pale-gold Chablis or Rhine wine with fish or chicken, and ruby Claret with your steak or roast

"Sweet" wines are made for serving with refreshments. When you're entertaining casually, try setting out small glasses of Muscatel. It's a popular golden wine richly endowed with the distinctive flavor of Muscat grapes

Wine advice, 1950s
California wine ads offered advice on serving wine as part of an education program to entice more Americans to drink wine.

The Turning Point

Stephen Spurrier was an English wine merchant living in Paris. He had tasted a number of California wines and was reasonably impressed, so in late 1975 he decided to visit the state. He returned to Paris converted. In May 1976, he introduced several respected French wine authorities to interesting California wines at a Paris tasting competition. Spurrier poured ten reds and ten whites, twelve of which were born and raised in northern California. He included a few "controls" in the samples—extraordinary French wines his judges would recognize—but all the bottles were masked for the "blind" testing. Spurrier hoped the judges would at least be as impressed as he was by what California produced. Even he was surprised by the results.

The top-rated red, a 1973 Cabernet Sauvignon from Warren and Barbara Winiarski's Stag's Leap Wine Cellars, and the white, a 1973 Chardonnay from Chateau Montelena, were both from Napa. Two highly regarded French wines finished second in each category. It was the wine tasting heard round the world. In his book, *American Vintage: The Rise of American Wine,* author Paul Lukacs put it in context: "In America it inspired the wine industry to raise its standards and to begin thinking of 'world-class' as a goal, while in Europe, it led winemakers to look at American wine with a new appreciation and respect . . . that great wine could come from vineyards that did not have centuries of grape-growing history behind them. . . ." Fine wine no longer required historic dirt.

It was a distinctly American, even Californian, revelation. This nation commonly misquotes Henry Ford, who never said simply "History is bunk." But that attitude—that history *is* bunk—has not betrayed California's winemakers. The American melting pot brought countless ideas from numerous nationalities. People with open minds studied their lessons and moved on, adapting what worked and jettisoning what didn't. Winemakers beginning with Buena Vista's Agoston Haraszthy demonstrated, as Lukacs put it, "that their present success had little if anything to do with past accomplishment." This led to a willingness to trust science as a teacher, blend formal thinking with artistic interpretation, take risks, educate customers, and thereby raise the standards of all wine.

Intelligent modern winemakers such as Wild Horse Winery & Vineyards's Ken Volk in San Luis Obispo County create wine from a palette of flavors. Volk blends small percentages of historic grape varieties with popular favorites, aging them in precisely monitored mixes of new, one-, two-, and three-year-old American- or French-oak barrels. Though not always successful, this painstaking labor yields flavors at once silken smooth and mind-bendingly complex.

Jordan's Rob Davis in the Alexander Valley meticulously scans his Chardonnay grapes and his estate-harvested Cabernet grapes as they slowly

1973 Cabernet Sauvignon Napa Valley Stag's Leap Vineyards

STAG'S LEAP WINE CELLARS

Produced & bottled by Stag's Leap Wine Cellars, Napa, Calif. • Alcohol 13% by volume

Stag's Leap Wine Cellars
Wine merchant Stephen Spurrier held a taste test in Paris in 1976 pitting northern California wines against the best French wines. The surprise winners were a 1973 Chardonnay from Chateau Montelena and this 1973 Cabernet from Stag's Leap, both of Napa. The 1976 Paris tasting changed the way the world viewed California wines.

Stag's Leap Wine Cellars

Warren Winiarski moved to Napa from Chicago in 1964 and purchased a 50-acre prune orchard in the shadow of Stag's Leap Palisades, adding in 1972 more land and establishing his winery. When the fledgling Stag's Leap's Cabernet Sauvignon swept the 1976 Paris tasting, Winiarski remembered, "It was recognized that, although our wines might be different from the French, they shared the same degree of excellence, and both were judged by universal rather than regional standards."

Jordan Vineyard & Winery

Tom Jordan's winery outside Healdsburg in central Sonoma County is one of the county's most elegant. Inspired by central France's chateau architecture, Jordan called on San Francisco architects Backen Arrigoni & Ross to fulfill his vision. The result is a treat to the eye from any angle.

file across the sorting tables, watching for any grape that is not absolutely perfect. Where Volk produces a dozen varieties of red and white wine, Sonoma's Davis creates only one of each for owner Tom Jordan. Davis's critical attention to every phase yields pure flavors of unmatched smoothness and clarity.

Growers, such as Jeff Newton, who with his partner, Larry Finkle, manages some 1,200 acres of vineyards for seven Santa Barbara County wineries, carefully calculate their efforts and experiments. They travel in the winter to compare notes with progressive European growers and winemakers, and then come home to the sunny Santa Ynez Valley to adapt what fits, experiment with what might, and eliminate what hasn't. Matching vineyard row width to vine aggressiveness and heartiness gives Newton's clients—including Dan Gainey, Pierre Lafond, Tom Stolpman, and Santa Barbara Winery—a variety of flavors to blend into an assortment of wines.

And on an awe-inspiring scale, ranch manager Bill Petrovik keeps track of Monterey County's San Bernabe, an 8,400-acre vineyard first established in 1973 by Prudential Insurance. Prudential planted the vineyard by market research, filling in acre after acre with what sold well—meaning, in those days, Cabernet and Zinfandel. But the area proved surprisingly cool, and the red grapes never fully ripened. The lesson they and others have learned was to plant what grows well, and when Manteca's Delicato Family Wines acquired the property, they replanted or grafted over vines mostly with white grapes. Petrovik has managed twenty-two harvests at San Bernabe, and he knows pretty well what can grow where. He raises twenty-two varieties of grapes, including Pinot Blanc, Malvesia Bianco, Chardonnay, white Riesling, and Chenin Blanc, on the world's largest vineyard, a property that stretches nearly seven miles and boasts twenty-one definable micro-climates. Delicato uses about 20 percent of the vineyard's grapes. He has a client list for the rest of the vineyard output that Petrovik says would make a knowledgeable visitor gape. He knows they come to San Bernabe from all over the state for the variety, to give their wines greater complexity and more interesting flavor.

And flavor, as Paris wine seller Stephen Spurrier showed the world back in 1976, is what gets attention. It keeps customers coming back.

Napa vineyards
"Plant grapes," a young Julio Gallo advised in 1931. Visionaries such as Gallo and others foresaw an end to Prohibition and the establishment of a strong California wine industry. This vineyard grows at ZD Wines north of the city of Napa.

Chapter Two

Grape Varieties

What Grows Where and
What You Make of It

California is not France. And what has worked in France for growing grapes and making wine for years, centuries even, may never work in California.

The French believe in the concept of *terroir*, a mystical amalgam of climate, soil, and exposure—to sun, rain, gray skies, blue skies—that is a fundamental influence on grape growing and winemaking. Because the French have been crafting wines for centuries, they have analyzed the soils everywhere. They have learned, for example, that Pinot Noir grapes thrive in soils rich in limestone.

The winemakers of California have written new rules in their understanding of a distinctly Californian sense of *terroir*. For one thing, there is little limestone in California, and yet Pinot Noir grapes do extremely well in many places throughout the state. Soil analyses of successful California plots, in some cases, contradict what French analyses indicate should work. Again, it's part of that Californian attitude of independent, open-minded flexibility.

And California is not France. Americans eat different food and eat it differently; we drink wine differently, as well. American winemakers have come to believe that European winemaking traditions, which have created the finest Burgundy and Bordeaux wines, have also hidebound them to their own rules and rigidity.

In his book, *The Wines of California,* author Stephen Brook summarized it well: "Bordeaux, with its leaner, tougher, more mineral wines, most of them demanding quite a few years in the cellar to shed their tannins and attain their unmatched elegance, has established a style that California can't really aspire to. Bordeaux wears neck-ties, has impeccable manners, and secures its [shirtsleeve] cuffs with silver links. California Cabernet likes to take its shirt off, head for the beach in a . . . convertible, and chase girls."

Some California winemakers have tried for years to produce true Bordeaux and Burgundy wines, but have not gotten too much closer to the French originals. To wine critics and observers such as the influential Robert M. Parker Jr. of the *Wine Advocate,* this is not at all a bad thing. Parker celebrates and encourages the irony that many contemporary wine writers have noticed in the past several years: French winemakers are becoming more Californian, producing wines that are more easily drinkable when young, and that deliver richer, more voluptuous flavors at any stage.

Previous page:
Cabernet Sauvignon vines
Cabernet Sauvignon grapes grow on the grounds of Jordan Vineyard & Winery near Healdsburg.

Autumn vineyard colors
Fall is perhaps the most beautiful time to visit Napa and Sonoma Counties. Harvest starts in early September, and days can be hot. By mid October, traffic has diminished, temperatures have dropped, and millions of vines are beginning to turn colors. In Carneros, this Robert Mondavi vineyard sparkles in late-afternoon sun.

Growing Grapes and Making Wines

Winemakers around the globe agree that it is indeed possible to make bad wine from good grapes yet it is not possible to make good wine from bad grapes. Others have learned that planting good grape stock in the wrong soil or climate conditions cannot yield good grapes.

Concessions in grape growing and winemaking lead to a compromised wine. Great wine-grape stock in marginally incorrect climate or soil, or in the hands of an amateur winemaker, yields less-than-great wine. As Philip Wagner points out in his valuable book, *A Wine-Grower's Guide,* "Certain varieties . . . if grown in a region that suits them, may always be counted on to produce good sound agreeable ordinary wines. The grape varieties that go into most of California's bulkwines, such as Carignane, Colombard, Grenache, Zinfandel [and] Barbera . . . in the very best locations may even produce wine better than ordinary.

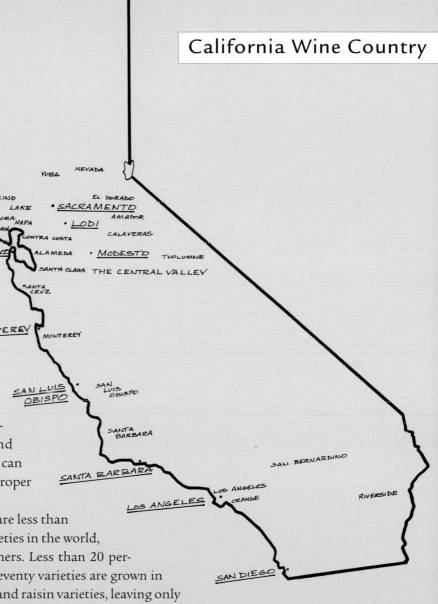

California Wine Country

"There exist a limited number of grape varieties," Wagner continues, "most of them rather shy bearers, all of them choosy as to climate and inclined to be particular as to soil, which are the source of the truly fine wines . . . the most famous of all being those called Pinot Noir, Cabernet Sauvignon, Chardonnay, Riesling and Semillon. In Europe they are the sources, respectively, of the greatest of the red Burgundies, the Clarets, the white Burgundies, the wines commonly called Rhine and Moselle, and the Sauterns." All of these grapes can be used to make fine wines when grown in the proper *terroir* of California.

Grapes belong to the species *Vitis.* There are less than sixty species of grapes yet more than 8,000 varieties in the world, many of them indistinctly separated from others. Less than 20 percent are cultivated and perhaps only sixty or seventy varieties are grown in California. Of these, a number are table-grape and raisin varieties, leaving only some thirty-six red-wine and twenty-four white-wine grape types grown and harvested for winemaking.

Of the sixty grape species, one is of principal interest to California winemakers and their customers, *Vitis vinifera.* First known as the "old world" grape, *Vitis vinifera* is now called the American, or Californian, grape. This species thrives in California weather. *Vitis vinifera* also survives in Midwestern and Eastern vineyards until they freeze; a 10-degree-Fahrenheit "hard freeze" splits the vine, killing it.

California Red-Wine Grape Varietals

Cabernet Sauvignon grapes

Pinot Noir grapes

Primary Red-Wine Grapes

Cabernet Sauvignon: The cooler the climate, the better for growing Cabernets. They develop a strong aroma that evolves into a rich bouquet in complete fermentation and good aging. Aging is a necessary part of the process with Cabs, because it tames the tannin within the grapes. Some makers bottle Cabernet grapes unblended with others, as the finest French Claret makers do. This is the stuff of the finest California wines.

Merlot: Often bottled by itself as a varietal, Merlot grapes are also used in blends with Cabernet Sauvignon to smooth them out and bring Cabs to bottling readiness sooner.

Petite Sirah: Typically known as Syrah in France and Shiraz in Australia, these grapes produce red wines of deep color and heavy body. They can also be somewhat rough with a none-too-delicate bouquet. An acquired taste, their loyalists are fierce, and many Petite Sirahs make excellent wines.

Pinot Noir: There are more than a thousand clones of Pinot and not all produce great wine. Pinot ripens early. Growers and winemakers in cool regions who take care are producing fine Pinots, and it's an enjoyable experiment finding the good ones.

Sangiovese: This versatile Italian grape is famous as one of the varietals blended to create light- and medium-bodied Chianti as well as the refined Brunello di Montalcino. Widely planted in California by the many pioneering Italian wineries in the early 1900s, it's now making a comeback in impressive new wines.

Zinfandel: In the coolest regions, Zinfandels produce brilliant, delicious, rich-bodied wines with their recognizable bouquet. In warmer regions, these grapes produce a flatter, heavier flavor that works quite well in jug wines.

Secondary Red-Wine Grapes

Barbera: This well-known Italian red produces a distinct aroma as a grape (grapes have aromas that ideally diminish during the winemaking process; wines have bouquet that, ideally, increase over time.) Barbera wines are heavy bodied, well balanced, and if well aged, can exhibit good character.

Cabernet Franc: This French grape from the Bourdeaux region creates aromatic wines. It is often blended with the harsher Cabernet Sauvignon to soften a wine.

Carignan: This grape produces wine of good color and body and clean flavor but with little character. It is generally used in blends, and in hotter regions, this is what it is intended for.

Gamay: Also known as the Beaujolais grape, Gamay produces soft, good-bodied wine with a fruity bouquet. It is best aged one to three years. There are several Gamay clones throughout California, producing better or lesser grapes.

Malbec: This old French red grape is most commonly blended with Cabernet grapes to soften the Cabs and shorten the aging time. It is relatively new in California but its acreage is growing.

Mission: These grapes are no longer used much because their grape color is not deep enough, sugar content too high, and acidity too low to make good-tasting red wine. However, these grapes are ideal for sherry and are making a comeback for producing sherry.

Nebbiolo: The Italians make great wines with this grape in the Piedmont district around Alba. Nebbiolo produces wine with a distinctive bouquet, a bit more tannin even than Cabernet Sauvignon, and what one expert calls "a special indescribable lusciousness." In the past decade it has been planted by inventive winemakers.

Refosco: This grape yields wine with a bit more tannin than most, but with good body and an agreeable aroma that evolves into a better bouquet after aging. This grape holds sufficient acidity even in very warm climates to produce distinctly superior wines.

Tinta Madiera: This high-sugar, moderate-acidity dry-wine grape is mostly used for smooth, delicate ports.

California White-Wine Grape Varietals

Primary White-Wine Grapes

Chardonnay: In the cool regions, these legendary white-wine grapes develop a near-perfect balance of acid and sugar. They have been used to produce the finest dry white wines of California.

Chenin Blanc: This is California's second-most widely planted white wine grape. It produces wines that are slightly sweet, fruity, and light.

Sauvignon Blanc grapes

Chardonnay grapes

Sauvignon Blanc: This delicious grape produces a high sugar content with a distinctive flavor and aroma that develops the best California Sauternes, the aromatic and slightly bitter dry wines. It is also frequently blended with Semillon to produce a dry white wine.

White Riesling: Rieslings thrive in the humidity of central Europe under cooler skies more often gray than blue. In California, Riesling grapes can overripen even in Region II conditions, developing too much sugar and dropping acidity too low to produce wines of the type Europeans and world travelers have come to love. Rieslings made in the coolest California climates come the closest to the European delicacy and flavor.

Secondary White-Wine Grapes

Colombard: This is one of the few hot-climate white grapes yielding enough acidity to make good wines. It is often blended with less-acidic varieties. Alone or blended, it produces refreshing, clean flavors.

Muscat Canelli: In Italy, this grape is used to produce Asti Spumante, the sparkling, sweet muscatel. In California, this also yields grapes to create fine, sweet muscats.

Pinot Blanc: Sometimes confused with Chardonnay, the Pinot Blanc grapes develop a similarly strong aroma with what some call a "stony" flavor. Wines made from grapes grown in cooler regions can nearly match Chardonnays in appeal.

Semillon: This grape needs moderate heat for successful flavor development. While it is high in sugar, it is not high in acidity. Proper fermentation is important. By itself, Semillon yields a naturally sweet wine; blended, with Sauvignon Blanc, it can create a fine dry white.

Sylvaner: These grapes produce wines of good character with a nice balance of acidity and sugar that usually are drunk young. They are often delicate. In the Rhine, Moselle, and Alsace regions of Germany, Sylvaners are the house wines of many better hotels and inns.

Viognier: This Rhône grape gives wines a fruity flavor and golden color.

Chapter Three

A Year in the Life of a Winery

How Fine Wine is Made

The Grape Harvest

In the old days, winemakers made wine in the winery. They took in whatever grapes crossed their threshold and worked to make the best of them. Those were not necessarily the *good* old days, if modern winemakers have anything to say about history.

Today, winemakers visit the vineyards regularly. They talk with their growers, whether on their own estates or on contract vineyards where independent growers raise fruit for them. And when harvest begins, hands-on winemakers such as Niebaum-Coppola's Scott McLeod, Wild Horse's Ken Volk, Fiddlehead Cellars's Kathy Joseph, and many others do the "one hundred berry sample" every morning during harvest, noting and pulling fruit randomly from vines throughout the blocks. They test sugar content, measured with a refractometer in degrees Brix; this helps them know when to go ahead with harvesting their grapes or when to hold off.

When it's a go, activities get frantic. For the 2000 fall harvest, McLeod walked along with his harvesters, inspecting vine by vine the grapes they were harvesting. St. Helena had been hammered with 100-plus-degree heat for a week, and he was worried that some fruit had gotten "sunburned." His pickers harvested these sun-exposed grapes separately so any burnt flavor wouldn't taint the other fruit. Near Lompoc in Santa Barbara County, Kathy Joseph rode the tractor-drawn gondolas as her crews harvested her Pinot Noir grapes. She personally culled the less-than-perfect grapes from her harvest.

These two young, intelligent winemakers are not unique, and the best winemakers now proclaim that great winemaking begins in the vineyards with great farming.

Harvest begins when grapes have fully ripened and reached their optimum flavor, usually in late August to early November. Winemakers determine this partially by measuring sugar content, ideally for reds, between 22 and 27 degrees Brix. (This ferments down to 12 to 14 percent alcohol, calculated by multiplying Brix by 0.55.) Growers harvest white wine grapes at less sugar content than red, seeking an optimum of 21 to 25 degrees Brix, that will result in wine of 11.5 to 14 percent alcohol.

Winemakers hope for dry harvests. A little rain is not bad and, in Northern California, not unusual. But too much interrupts the ripening cycle, dropping sugar. It can induce mold and mildew, and on thin-skinned grapes such as Pinot Noir, a hard rain can even shatter the grapes.

There are many styles of harvest. Some heartier grapes with stronger skins can be harvested with machines that literally shake the grape clusters lose from the vines. These machines start work hours before dawn while the grapes are juicy and at their firmest. At the other extreme is the harvest at Robert Mondavi's Opus One in Oakville. Opus One pickers harvest its Cabernet grapes in tens of thousands of shallow yellow trays where clusters lie only one row deep. Such lavish care—at harvest and year round—ensures Opus One of superb fruit to make its $100-per-bottle wines.

Previous page:

Harvest
Jordan Vineyard & Winery occupies nearly 1,200 acres east of Healdsburg, of which only about 130 acres are planted in Cabernet Sauvignon grape blocks. Owner Tom Jordan has recently added olive trees. Countless native oak trees cover Jordan's rolling hilly property.

Picking grapes
Kathy Joseph, owner and winemaker of Fiddlehead Cellars, climbs one of her rows during the harvest of Pinot Noir grapes in her Santa Barbara County vineyard.

The value of speed

At Jordan Vineyard & Winery, the harvest pickers know the value of speed. The freshest grapes provide the finest juice, and the harvesters are paid by the number of tubs they fill. Full tubs contain forty to fifty pounds of grapes, and pickers hustle from sunrise to mid afternoon. Crews of ten to twelve harvesters work on two or three rows on either side of the gondolas. During their eight-hour workday, they'll toss these forty pound tubs a hundred times, picking two tons of grapes each.

Dressing warm

In the dawn chill, warmly dressed harvesters at Stolpman Vineyards begin to pick Viognier grapes that Stolpman ships north to several Napa winemakers. One secret of surviving harvest is layering clothes. Workday temperatures begin below 50 degrees and by mid morning can top 80 degrees.

Processing the Grapes

Once at the winery, the grapes are sorted to remove clusters that are overripe, rotten, or unripe and to pull out leaves, stems, bugs, and other foreign matter. This is done over slow-moving rubber-belted conveyors, and here a critical winemaker such as Jordan's Rob Davis stands by, watching sharply and occasionally jabbing his hand in among his other five sorters to catch something they missed.

This conveyor dumps the selected grapes into the presses. Most wineries now are using European-style bladder presses that use a rotating drum with thousands of narrow slits to drain the juice. That juice is squeezed out by an inflatable bag inside the drum.

Sorting grapes
At Charles Krug's Carneros vineyards, a sorter culls leaves and inferior grapes from the vineyard's harvest of Pinot Noir.

Tractoring grapes to the winery
Wild Horse's 3.2-acre block of Blau Frankisch yielded twelve tons of fruit from its first harvest, a quantity that pleased Ken Volk. Wild Horse grows a wide variety of grapes on its vineyards surrounding the winery.

Inspecting grapes
Charles Krug winemaker Jack Colaiaco, in the white shirt, watches as his winery sorters give one last inspection to Chardonnay grapes harvested hours earlier. Colaiaco set a target of 23.5 degrees Brix for his grapes, and he pays each supplier based on reaching that goal, giving them less if grapes are too high or too low.

The Fermentation Process

Generally, California winemakers ferment their red wines for five to twenty-five days. Most are fermented with their skins, meaning the juices soak in open-top stainless-steel tanks, mingling with the grape skins and the pulp or meat. There are natural yeasts in these skins that convert the grape's sugar into alcohol. What's more, with some reds, particularly the Sirah and Pinot Noir grapes, some winemakers leave some stems in to supplement the tannin, although this practice has fallen from favor as others discovered this also added an astringency to the flavor that no one wanted.

Fermentation does not always begin, or end, smoothly. It can actually get "stuck," meaning the process gets so far and then stops. Some winemakers add nutrients or substances such as Superfood to start or restart the fermentation. Throughout this process, depending on the color of wine the makers want to achieve, they follow one or several procedures. One is called "pumping over," where, literally, they drain off juice from the bottom of the tank and pour it back over the skins that have floated to the surface, forming what is called a "grape cap." The second technique is known as "punch down," where a winemaker uses a plunger to force the cap down through the juice.

As fermentation concludes and the sugar content or Brix approaches zero, some winemakers add diamonium phosphate, a nitrogen additive used to boost fermentation to conclusion. Once fermentation is complete, the grapes, or "must," and the "free run" juice are separated. The must is pressed again to obtain the last juices that will be more tannic and bitter. What remains is called the "pomace." This press-juice sometimes gives winemakers another flavor with which to develop their finished products.

To make their white wines, winemakers keep the grape juice away from the skins for white wines to avoid any color taint. After de-stemming, the grapes are crushed and quickly drained into stainless-steel tanks or oak barrels and are chilled for fermentation. The grape skins and meat are generally pressed a second time. Sometimes this juice is added to the first pressing; other times it is sold to other winemakers or it is used by the original winemaker in some of the "second label" wines. The juice clarifies naturally as sediments and bacterial settle to the bottom. Because there is no skin, there is neither a pump-over or punch-down phase.

Cellarmasters either add yeast or allow the wine to begin fermentation from its own natural yeasts. Makers know to age Chardonnays and Sauvignon Blanc grapes from six to fourteen months in oak, often on the lees, leaving the sediment in the bottom of the barrel to subtly influence the flavor. However, they ferment and age Chenin Blanc, Gewürztraminer, and Rieslings in stainless steel in order to avoid oak flavor introduction and preserve the freshness. Some winemakers induce secondary malolactic fermentation, others do not. It is a stylistic decision.

Fermenting

Michelle MacCready punches down Sierra Vista Winery's Syrah grapes that have been fermenting for two weeks in this four-foot-tall tank. Called an open-top fermenter, one advantage it offers is ease in pressing the grape skins and meat repeatedly through the juice to impart additional flavor and color to the juice.

Preparing fermentation tanks

Buena Vista Carneros cellarworker Leon Towon installs racking valves in the winery's fermentation tanks. Cellar staff work their longest days in the weeks during and after harvest as fermentation turns the grape's sugar into alcohol, a delicate process. Six-day weeks are common and a seventh day is not unusual.

Top left:
Final press

After weeks of fermentation, winemakers do a final press of the pomace, the wet pulp or grape skins, meat, and whatever stems were not caught by de-stemming procedures. Here Michelle MacCready releases the pomace from the sides of Sierra Vista's bladder press. Wineries sometimes blend the juice extracted from this process with their initial "free-run" juice. If not, it either becomes their "second label" wines or they sell it to bulk-wine producers.

Top right:
Monitoring fermentation

At Buena Vista Carneros, oenologist Jason Mackura monitors fermentation of Zinfandel grapes harvested from its Rocky Terrace Vineyards. Harvest is a frantic time in all wineries as the agriculture of grape growing metamorphoses into the science of fermentation and finally into the art and industry of winemaking.

Crafting Wine Barrels

Seguin Moreau Tonnellerie of Napa is an Old World cooperage that supplies oak barrels to wineries. Oak barrels weigh 100 pounds empty and hold between 225 and 228 liters, which was historically regarded as the amount of wine a vineyard worker could process in a day. The barrels do not come cheap. Barrels made from American oak cost $350 each whereas French-oak barrels cost $600. This is because American oak can be easily sawn, making production easier and less expensive; French oak must be split to respect the grain, requiring more wood to make a single barrel.

Closing the barrel

Open fires are a key ingredient in barrel making. At this stage of closing the barrel, workers wrap a cable attached to a slow-turning winch around the splayed out staves. Using heat and repeated light sprays of water, the cable draws back into the winch, helping warp the barrel closed.

Adjusting barrel staves

Master barrelmaker Andrew Byars, a native of London, England, raises the staves on a French-oak barrel at Seguin Moreau Tonnellerie in Napa. Byars selects thirty to thirty-six pieces, using a mix of large, medium, and small sizes. Large, wider staves provide strength while the smaller, narrower pieces allow for the barrel's curvature.

Barrel repair

If a customer's barrel springs a leak, Seguin Moreau can repair it, even if they didn't built it originally. Master cooper Ramiro Herrera completes a repair. Here he slices a notch into the new stave so the original lid fits tightly.

Making barrel heads

Master cooper Douglas Rennie, a native of Glasgow, Scotland, gained years of experience making barrels for whiskey distillers before coming to Seguin Moreau. He puts finishing touches on a replacement barrel head for a customer's repair.

Above:
Barrel toasting

Barrel toasting, or carmelization, is a critical stage, and winemakers order barrels specifying light, medium, or heavy toast. The more carmelization, the more the wine can penetrate the oak, inducing more tannins and stronger flavors to the aging wine. Fire tenders use scraps from weather-aged oak used for barrel staves. French-oak barrels impart a less "oaky" flavor to aging wines and are most popular for white wines. American oak, with its fuller flavor, is preferred for the big Zinfandels and Cabernet Sauvignons. Light toasting requires forty minutes over the floor fire. Heavy toasting takes about eighty minutes.

Aging the Wine

Winemakers age their red wine either in upright temperature-controlled stainless-steel tanks or in oak barrels. Where the stainless imparts no new flavor to the wine and some winemakers prefer that, others use a variety of new, used, French- and American-made barrels to further mature their flavors. Sometime during this stage, before or after going into wood tanks, red wines go through a second fermentation, called malolactic that converts the crisp, tart malic acid into softer lactic acid.

Winemakers move wine from barrel to barrel, aerating and clarifying the wine in a process known as "racking." The clarifying process occurs as drained wines leave behind their sediment and post-fermentation bacteria, jointly called the "lees." The trend now is to not filter the finest wines. Filtration removes that last sediment but some winemakers believe it also takes an edge off the flavor and complexity. Not filtering leaves the wines slightly cloudy, and there is a risk that unfiltered bacteria growing in the bottle can ruin the wine. To avoid that, some winemakers add sulfer dioxide, which eliminates the bacteria. Most red wines are, however, "fined" by adding gelatin, whipped egg whites, or other substances that coagulate sediments into heavier masses that settle to the bottoms of the barrels.

Near the end of the process, some winemakers will blend their Cabernet Sauvignon, Merlot, Zinfandel, or Sangiovese wines with others such as Malbec, Petite Verdo, and Cabernet Franc to create the classic Bordeaux flavors. Pinot Noir is so delicate that it is rarely blended, its flavors altering noticeably with even the slightest additions of other wines. The blending process is the final step in what makes the wines each winery's customers favor. What to blend and when to blend it helps define the maker's taste and the winery's products.

The last phase is bottling. Winemakers may hold the finished bottle for as long as three years or they might ship immediately.

To make their white wines, winemakers rarely blend Chenin Blanc, Riesling, or Gewürztraminer and age them only a short time before bottling and selling them. Their flavor is best when young and fresh. The Sauvignon Blanc and Semillon are often blended, depending on which flavor the makers wish to emphasize. Winemakers rarely blend a Chardonnay.

Most wineries fine their white wines by adding a powdery clay called bentonite. This coagulates around the excess proteins and settles to the bottom, clarifying the wine. Then the wines are stabilized at 30 degrees Fahrenheit to remove excess potassium bitartrate (also known as cream of tartar), the substance added to the soil in the vineyard that gives wine the acidity it needs to create a balanced flavor that is neither too sour or too sweet.

White wines are then racked, pumped from one barrel to another, then to another, just as the reds are, to remove the lees. Makers add sulfur dioxide at this point, to protect against bacteria. A short while later, the winery bottles the white wines, and generally these reach the market within six months.

Filling the barrels

Freshly pressed Cabernet Sauvignon runs from the barrel press through pumps and hoses into oak barrels in Livingston Moffett's caves. The winery uses almost 100 percent French-oak barrels except for its Stanley Wine that is aged in a mix of French- and American-oak barrels.

Checking the aging progress

Winemaker Etienne Cowper tastes Mount Palomar Winery's port. Mount Palomar ages this sweet wine in sun-drenched oak barrels outside the winery in Temecula in Riverside County. Using a device called a "wine thief," Cowper siphons a taste from each of dozens of barrels of port. He tastes for mature flavor, then marks the barrels. He's looking for those he'll blend immediately and those to leave for another month or longer.

Cleaning fermentation tanks

Cellar master Karl Wicka finishes his clean-up of one of Wild Horse's fermentation tanks in the winery. Steam rises from the nearly scalding hot water used to sanitize every surface that comes in contact with the juice. Sanitation is good winemaking.

The Fall and Winter Months

Ideally, the weather cooperates year round. Growers and winemakers love plenty of rain in fall and winter after harvest. Pruning begins a month or two after harvest. In the spring, they want mild temperatures that encourage their vines to bud and set healthy grape clusters; an unseasonable frost can kill buds and entire vines. And they want mild to warm summers with temperatures building gradually with no brutal hot or cold snaps.

Pruning

Pruning removes living canes, shoots, and leaves, making it easier to control weeds, diseases, and insects. It also reduces the number of grape clusters, thereby improving fruit flavor and yield at harvest.

Top:

Planting new vines

At Fiddlehead Cellars, workers plant French Pinot Noir vines. Growers Jeff Newton and Larry Finkle settled on seven-foot-wide rows with four-foot spacing, using six different clones on four different rootstocks. But it's no guessing game; experience from other parts of the same vineyard tells them exactly what works best and what to expect from every square foot.

Bottom:

Grapevine buds

Bud-break signals the beginning of this Pinot Noir grapevine's growing season at Fiddle-head Cellars.

Chapter Four

Napa County

America's Most Prized Appellation

Napa Valley, for all its influence in the wine world, is barely thirty miles long, stretching northwest from the city of Napa up to Calistoga. There are two routes to get from one end to the other, California Highway 29 and Silverado Trail. During grape harvest, from late August to late October, traffic on both these roads lumbers along behind loaded grape gondolas towed behind tractors and tandem truck trailers heading from any of the valley's vineyards to its more than 200 wineries. And during summer, traffic slows to accommodate the valley's other industry, tourism, as thousands drive in to sample Napa's wine, food, and hospitality.

Not all of Napa's—or even California's—wineries are lavish. Many of the state's fine wines come from small farms where the owners' families serve multiple roles. One such operation is Livingston Moffett Winery in St. Helena. John and Diane (née Moffett) Livingston raise six acres of Cabernet, Chardonnay, and Sirah grapes on their ten-acre ranch in front of their updated farmhouse in the hills southwest of town. They bought their property in 1975, looking for a place to raise their children, but they mostly ignored the vines growing around them.

It wasn't until the early 1980s when family friend and winemaker Randy Dunn at Caymus in Rutherford pointed out that their vineyard was on the Rutherford "bench," a similarity shared with the fine Caymus wines he produced. Dunn helped John Livingston change careers and bring the vineyard back to life, advising the couple through their first six vintages. Now, another nine harvests later, the Livingstons produce 5,000 cases annually. For such a small winery—though it's far from the state's smallest—modest-scale and unusual promotional methods are one way to gain public attention.

In each of the past ten years, the Livingstons have sent out invitations in August for their late-September Harvest Party. It began as a weekend-long party for their oldest son Trent's college buddies but has developed into a tradition to which a number of valued clients are invited. Everybody who comes picks grapes, no exceptions. John usually leaves an acre of Cabernet for the eighty or so guests to harvest.

People begin arriving Friday afternoon, in time to swim or play tennis, greet friends, and enjoy a huge pasta feast. Most of the invitees come from San Francisco but many drive up from Los Angeles, and one couple recently flew in from Boston. They camp out in tents on the farmhouse's front lawn overlooking the vineyard and the valley. Picking begins the next morning after a quick breakfast and strong coffee. Each of the eighty guests is expected to pick four bucketloads of forty to fifty pounds of grapes, amounting to four tons. Everyone scrambles through the vineyards, learning, generally without incident, to aim the razor-sharp curved knives away from themselves as they cut grape clusters from the vines.

Picking—at a much slower pace than the professional harvesters—winds up after lunch, and guests can either relax or help with the sort and crush through the afternoon. Those still game help with rack over, pumping earlier-harvested juice from tanks into the Livingstons' barrels. Primarily they use 100 percent French oak barrels, though one of their wines, Stanley, is aged in 65 percent American and 35 percent French oak.

The evening ends with a lavish barbecue during which John, Diane,

Napa Selection
From left to right: Pine Ridge 1997 Howell Mountain Cabernet Sauvignon; Beringer 1999 Napa Valley Chardonnay Appellation Collection; Beringer 1997 Napa Valley Cabernet Sauvignon; Livingston 1998 Moffett Napa Valley Chardonnay; Niebaum-Coppola 1998 Carneros Chardonnay Director's Reserve; Niebaum-Coppola 1998 Rutherford Merlot; Niebaum-Coppola 1999 Rutherford Zinfandel.

and Trent pour new wines and preview what they'll be bottling the next spring. The Livingstons make a minimal charge on their working guests, to cover the wines they pour and the food they serve. No one ever complains.

Livingston is open year round but only by appointment.

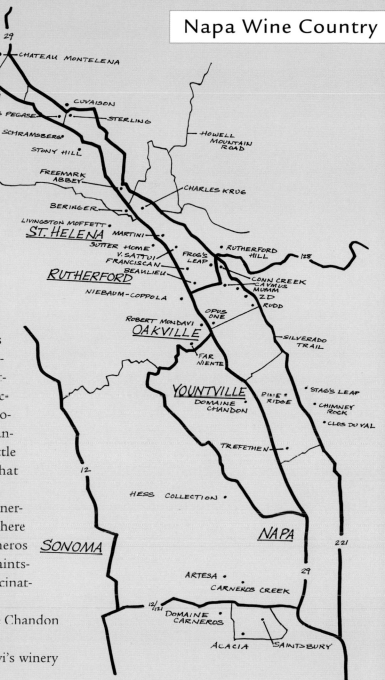

Napa Valley Institutions

At the other end of the promotion spectrum is the Napa Valley Wine Auction. First held in 1981, it is a fund-raising benefit for local medical healthcare, taking place during the first weekend of June. Since it began, the auction has raised more than $25 million for its worthy recipients. The three-day event ranges from small, intimate dinners and tastings with local chefs and winemakers on Thursday and Friday to a feast at Meadowood Resort in St. Helena on Saturday evening, and culminates with silent and live auctions on Sunday. During the 2000 auction, generous donors paid $1,800 per couple for admission and raised another $9 million. Included in the auction was one bottle of Oakville Screaming Eagle Cabernet Sauvignon that brought $500,000.

Napa is populated with some of America's best wineries. In the Carneros District west of the city of Napa, there are Acacia Winery, Artesa Vineyards & Winery, Carneros Creek, champagne-maker Domaine Carneros, and Saintsbury. Further north is the Hess Collection with its fascinating art collection.

Traveling north to Yountville, there are Domaine Chandon and Trefethen.

In Oakville, visit Far Niente and Robert Mondavi's winery as well as his masterpiece Opus One.

In the Rutherford area, you will find the Niebam-Coppola Estate Winery and Beaulieu Vineyards as well as Turley Cellars, founded by Larry Turley and Frog's Leap Winery's John Williams.

Around St. Helena, there are Franciscan Estates, Livingston Moffett Winery, and V. Sattui Winery. And don't forget Sutter Home, who, as one fellow Napa Valley winemaker put it, "deserves huge credit for their White Zinfandel, a more user-friendly wine, like a McIntosh apple, that got new wine drinkers to try the beverage and learn about other wines because of it."

In the Calistoga area, visit Clos Pegase, Chateau Montelena of the 1976 Paris winetasting fame, and Diamond Creek Vineyards, whose limited production includes California's most expensive Cabernet at $300 per bottle.

Along Silverado Trail traveling from south to north, there are Clos du Val, Chimney Rock, Pine Ridge, the well-known Stag's Leap Wine Cellars, Rudd Estate, ZD Wines, champagne-maker Mumm Napa Valley, Caymus, Conn Creek, Frog's Leap, Rutherford Hill, the historic Charles Krug Winery, Sterling, and Cuvaison.

Napa's Architectural Wonders

For architecture lovers, there is much to see and enjoy in Napa, both old and new. Classic architecture is best experienced at Beringer Vineyards, Freemark Abbey, and Charles Krug in St. Helena; Chateau Montelena in Calistoga; Francis Ford Coppola's Niebaum-Coppola Estate Winery in Rutherford (the old Inglenook Winery); and Far Niente in Oakville.

For Napa's striking modern architecture, don't miss the much-photographed Clos Pegase in Calistoga, designed by celebrated architect Michael Graves.

The collaboration between Robert Mondavi and Baron Philippe de Rothschild of Chateau Mouton Rothschild fame in Bordeaux has created the startling Opus One. Designed by Scott Johnson, the building is a visually entertaining blend of ageless classical and strikingly modern design.

Equally marvelous is Dominus Estate in Yountville, a structure sheathed in loose basaltic rock over steel, concrete, and glass, retained by fine steel mesh. Outside, the walls look ready to burst; inside, the effect is fanciful with daylight sifting past rocks through windows into the hallways and interior courtyards.

Also worthy of architectural note is Sterling Vineyards in Calistoga, whose design blends Moorish and Greek styles. Sterling is perched on a hilltop so its vineyards make most efficient use of the valley floors. Visitors reach the winery and tasting rooms only on a cable car (handicap access is available), and this pleasant ride up and down is worth half the cost of admission. While many vineyards and wineries offer guided or self-directed tours, Sterling's is one of the best with excellent signs. Take a sweater even on the warmest day; the tour passes through brisk, air-conditioned barrel rooms several times where there is much to read.

Livingston Moffett Winery
Late September brings good friends and the best customers to St. Helena for Livingston Moffett's Harvest Party. Guests arrive late Friday, and many pitch tents on John and Diane Livingston's front lawn. On Saturday the guests harvest grapes in the morning and help with the crush after lunch.

Livingston Moffett Winery
Learning the technique quickly, Carolyn Chandler of Santa Barbara filled her first bucket of Livingston estate Cabernet Sauvignon grapes. Each of the eighty guests is expected to harvest four such buckets—about 200 pounds in all—to clear the last acre of vines and empty the vineyard of its last ripe grapes.

Napa Valley Landmarks

Finally, no trip to Napa Valley would be complete without a visit to Robert Mondavi Winery, located on the west side of Highway 29 in Oakville. Mondavi has become the senior statesman among California winemakers. In 1966, he built the first new winery in California after Prohibition. He acquired the spectacular To-Kalon vineyards, one of Napa's oldest, and built a Spanish Mission–style complex designed by Cliff May, dedicated to tasting and educating. Among his newer ventures, Mondavi has opened a demonstration winery at Disneyland's new Disney's California Adventure theme park in Anaheim.

In addition, the ever-forward-looking Mondavi has acquired vineyards in southern France and, closer to home, has developed and generously contributed to the American Center for Wine, Food and the Arts. This thirteen-acre project incorporates agricultural and horticultural gardens, a superb café, exhibition spaces, food- and winetasting theaters, a film auditorium, and an outdoor amphitheater. Mondavi's interest in and encouragement of the center will continue his own winery's emphasis on education and tasting.

One more must-see for those interested in food is the spectacular Greystone Cellars winery building, originally the home of a county-wide cooperative that advanced winemakers cash for the wine they stored in Greystone's huge cellars. The Christian Brothers operated the winery for decades until the liquor conglomerate Heublein bought them out, taking the building in the acquisition. Now it is the home of the Culinary Institute of America's western facility that opened in August 1995. The facility teaches classes, gives tours, and boasts one of the valley's best culinary accessories and cookbook stores.

Lastly, in case you should finally tire of tasting great wine, two other Napa establishments are known for their fine California beverages. The mineral waters of both the Calistoga Mineral Water Company and the Crystal Geyser Water Company are drawn from the earth, bottled, and distributed in Calistoga.

Livingston Moffett Winery
Where harvesting grapes is mandatory for all guests, afternoon activities such as sorting are optional. But those who choose to participate get a good education in harvesting, sorting, de-stemming, and grape-crushing procedures. Most guests follow the grapes through the day.

Livingston Moffett Winery
Freshly harvested Cabernet grapes are stored in Livingston's caves, away from the warming noonday sunlight while John and Diane feed guests and friends a true farm lunch. The meal finished, John operates the forklift to move these 1,000-pound bins across the crush pad to the sorting table, and the work resumes.

Calistoga

Many travelers consider Napa County's village of Calistoga a destination in itself, regardless of its proximity to great wineries and beautiful vineyards. Nestled below its late-afternoon sunlit Palisades, Calistoga is well known for is thermal baths and its own Old Faithful geyser. Lining Lincoln Street, the main street in downtown Calistoga, are shops selling jewelry, books, souvenirs, clothing, artwork, and, of course, wine. On either side of the street and around the corners are also some of Napa County's better restaurants. Sports car drivers and motorcycle riders enjoy the roads of wine country. The county is also bicycle-friendly, and locals and visitors alike enjoy cycling Silverado Trail south from Calistoga.

Napa County

There is a direct relationship between healthy grape vines and healthy oak trees, and many growers go to great lengths to preserve the native oak trees throughout their vineyards. Oak woodlands are part of California's natural and cultural history, providing homes for hundreds of bird, mammal, snake, and reptile species, and for thousands of insect species as well as giving shade to grazing cattle.

Niebaum-Coppola Winery
Originally home to Gustave Niebaum's Inglenook Winery, the huge castle now houses Niebaum-Coppola and offers visitors tastes of fine red and white wines as well as a collection of motion-picture memorabilia from the films of owner Francis Ford and Eleanor Coppola. The Coppolas moved into St. Helena in 1975 when they acquired the back half of the large Inglenook winery. In 1995, they purchased the front half of the vineyard and the old chateau.

Niebaum-Coppola Winery
Harvesters at Niebaum-Coppola deal with tall, densely planted vines by using shallow trays (about the size of dishwashing tubs) rather than deep buckets, so they can toss them over the vines into waiting gondolas. Crews of ten to twelve harvesters work on two or three rows on either side of the gondolas at once. During their eight-hour workday, they'll toss these forty-pound tubs a hundred times, picking two tons of grapes each.

Niebaum-Coppola Winery
Winemaker Scott McLeod, center, carefully supervises harvest.

Domaine Chandon

The Carneros district straddles Napa and Sonoma Counties and is favored by cool, fog-laden breezes off the San Pablo Bay at the northern end of San Francisco Bay. Many of Napa and Sonoma's best winemakers grow some or all of their grapes here, as with this champagne-grape vineyard owned by Domaine Chandon.

Rain in the vineyards

Visiting Napa and Sonoma in the winter requires a raincoat and a warm sweater. The weather from December through March is cool and damp. Yet often moments after a rain, the sun bursts through, glinting off trellis lines and giving visitors unexpected views.

Culinary Institute of America

Once the home of the largest winemaking operation in California, Greystone Cellars now houses the Culinary Institute of America's western headquarters. The CIA teaches amateur students and professional chefs to dazzle their families and impress discriminating patrons all over the world.

Above images:

The French Laundry

Chef and owner Thomas Keller's five-star restaurant The French Laundry, in Yountville, is at the forefront of Napa Valley cuisine, along with other notable restaurants such as Tra Vigne, in St. Helena.

Charles Krug Winery

Two vineyard workers pick grapes during the autumn harvest.

Beringer Vineyards

St. Helena's Beringer boasts an elegant mansion. Frederick and Jacob Beringer were German, and their seventeen-room home was called Rhine House. However, because it was built in the 1880s during the reign of England's Queen Victoria, historians classify the huge structure as a Victorian.

Peju Province Winery
By January, leaves have fallen, and the vineyard calendar calls for pruning. At Rutherford's Peju Province Winery, a small crew trims vines by hand as the first of the wild mustard sprouts along the ground cover.

Rudd Estate
Along Silverado Trail, vineyard owner Leslie Rudd of Oakville has begun replanting his Cabernet Sauvignon and Chardonnay vines in tighter rows with narrower spacing between vines. Hoping to intensify the flavor in his grapes, Rudd reflects the statewide effort to further improve the quality of fruit that small- and medium-sized growers are producing.

Above:
Vineyards and mustard plants
After the fall rains, mustard plants often bloom alongside vineyards. This lovely plant is not native and is slightly invasive, yet most growers keep it to control winter erosion and because its visual appeal draws visitors to Napa and Sonoma. One story says Spanish missionaries introduced mustard as a spice for their meals and also to mark the trail between their missions. Another story says it arrived in soil used on ballast for sailing ships coming into San Francisco Bay in the 1850s with Gold Rush immigrants.

Yountville
From late spring through summer and into late fall, outdoor evening dining is one of the pleasures of visiting wine country. Here in Yountville in Napa County, patrons enjoy a summertime evening meal bathed in the warmth of the setting sun.

Madonna Estate Mont St. John
Madonna Estate Mont St. John is home to hundreds of old-growth Pinot Noir vines that change color like Vermont sugar maple trees as fall progresses. Mid fall is an ideal time to visit as most wineries have resumed tours after their hectic harvest schedules, yet hotel rooms are easily available.

Opus One
Striking architecture and stunning wine characterize Opus One, the collaboration between Napa's Robert Mondavi and France's Baron Philippe de Rothschild. Los Angeles architect Scott Johnson designed the building, completed in 1981. Opus One's neo-classical structures are almost hidden inside gentle, manicured berms giving passersby the clear impression that here, the vines and wine are most important.

Robert Mondavi Winery
Robert G. Mondavi and his eldest son, R. Michael Mondavi, founded Robert Mondavi Winery in 1966. The publicly traded company now comprises sixteen separate labels representing more than eighty wines from California, France, Italy, Australia, and Chile.

Above and left:

Clos Pegase Winery

One of Napa's architectural wonders is the much-visited and often-photographed Clos Pegase. Owners Jan and Mitsuko Shrem organized a national architecture competition to inspire the most striking and functional design. New Jersey architect Michael Graves established this Greco-Roman style as the design motif for the winery. Designed around a classical courtyard, Clos Pegase's public areas and private rooms also showcase the winery's collection and commitment to contemporary art. The winery opened in 1987 and has won dozens of major architectural awards. Mythology states that the winged horse Pegasus created not only the arts but also wine when his slashing hooves opened the Spring of the Muses. Its water fed the vines, creating the wine that ancient artists and poets consumed, inspiring their great works.

Charles Krug Winery

Charles Krug owners Peter Mondavi Sr. and son Peter Jr. discuss the harvest underway. Behind them, Krug's new, smaller-capacity tanks are part of efforts to elevate their wine's quality. In a common practice, they lease their larger tanks and barrels to neighboring wineries.

Chateau Montelena Winery

Before new barrels can be used, they must be tightened by swelling the wood. A cellar worker fills new oak barrels with hot water to tighten the wood's grain so they won't leak when winemaker Bo Barrett fills them with wine. Chateau Montelena uses nearly 2,000 barrels, which are housed in its caves inside the old castle and in nearby underground caves hollowed from the hillsides.

Sutter Home Winery

The Victorian mansion that is the headquarters of Sutter Home graces the city of St. Helena. The winery was founded in 1874 by Swiss-German immigrants and purchased by Italian immigrants John and Mario Trinchero in 1947. Still owned by the Trinchero family, Sutter Home has become one of America's best-selling wines.

Sterling Vineyards

Sterling Vineyards rests atop a 300-foot-high knoll near Calistoga, reached by cable car. Started in 1964, the winery was designed in the style of the white villages on the Greek island of Mykonos, a favorite destination of Sterling founder Englishman Peter Newton.

Domaine Carneros

In the heart of Napa's Carneros appellation, Domaine Carneros's French-style chateau houses the winery. Frenchman Claude Taittinger, president of Champagne Taittinger, fell in love with the beauty of northern California during his youthful travels and swore he would one day move back to the region. He established Domaine Carneros in 1989.

ZD Wines
The vines of ZD Wines, along Silverado Trail north of the city of Napa, begin to turn colors as harvest progresses. The visual sensation that the nearer rows are narrower is not a photographic trick; as growers seek the most efficient ways to produce superb fruit, they have replanted narrower rows to encourage vines to work harder to survive, which generally yields more-flavorful fruit.

Napa Valley's Best Wines and Wineries

Cabernet Sauvignons

B. R. Cohn Olive Hill
Beaulieu Private Reserve
Beringer Chabot
Cakebread Cellars
Caymus
Chateau Montelena Estate
Clos Pegase Hommage
Dominus
Dunn & Dunn Howell Mountain
Far Niente
Hess Collection
La Jota Cabernet Sauvignon and Cabernet
    Franc
Niebaum-Coppola
Opus One
Robert Mondavi Reserve
Robert Mondavi To-Kalon Estate Reserve
Screaming Eagle
Stag's Leap Wine Cellars

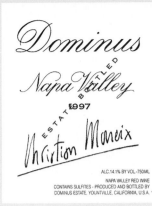

Chardonnays

Beringer Private Reserve
Franciscan
Hess Collection
Niebaum-Coppola
Robert Mondavi Reserve
Stony Hill
ZD Wines

Italian Wines

Beringer Sangiovese
Kent Rasmussen Sangiovese
Niebaum-Coppola
Robert Mondavi Barbera

Merlots

Beringer Chabot

Sparkling Wines

Domaine Chandon Reserve Brut
Mumm

Syrahs

Turley Cellars

Zinfandels

Howell Mountain
Robert Mondavi
Turley Cellars

Napa County Winery and Vineyard Resources

It is always wise to phone ahead before making your visit, to avoid disappointment. Sometimes facilities are closed to host private events. Always ask about tours; wineries sometimes suspend these during grape harvest or crush.

Don't be intimidated by the request to call for an appointment. Many of these are small wineries with few employees who are happy to meet you and share with you their wine and their knowledge. Calling for an appointment simply ensures someone will be there when you come to taste these fine wines.

Some wineries list tasting hours "by appointment only." Napa County issues a limited number of operating use permits for unlimited tasting. The rest of the county's wineries operate under "restricted use" regulations that allow tasting only by specific appointment.

Acacia Winery
2750 Las Amigas Road
Napa, CA 94559
707-226-9991
www.acaciawinery.com
Mon-Sat 10:00-4:30 by appointment
Sun 12-4:30 by appointment

Andretti Winery
4162 Big Ranch Road
Napa, CA 94558
707-255-3524
www.andrettiwinery.com
Daily 10:00-4:30

Artesa Vineyards & Winery
(formerly Codorníu Napa)
1345 Henry Road
Napa, CA 94558
707-224-1668
www.artesawinery.com
Daily 10-5

Beaulieu Vineyards
1960 St. Helena Highway
Rutherford, CA 94573
707-967-5230
www.bvwines.com
Daily 10-5 except major holidays

Beringer Vineyards
2000 Main Street
St. Helena, CA 94574
707-963-7115
www.beringer.com
Daily 9:30-5:30 tasting and tours

Carneros Creek Winery
1285 Dealy Lane
Napa, CA 94559
707-253-9463
www.carneroscreek.com
Daily 10-5

Caymus Vineyards
8700 Conn Creek Road
Rutherford, CA 94573
707-967-3010
www.caymus.com
Daily 10-4 by appointment only

Charles Krug Winery
2800 Main Street
St. Helena, CA 94574
707-967-2201
www.charleskrug.com
Daily 10:30-5:00

Chateau Montelena Winery
1429 Tubbs Lane
Calistoga, CA 94515
707-942-5105
www.montelena.com
Daily 10-4

Chimney Rock Winery
5350 Silverado Trail
Napa, CA 94558
707-257-2641
www.chimneyrock.com
Daily 10-5

Clos du Val Wine Company
5330 Silverado Trail
Napa, CA 94558
707-259-2225
www.closduval.com
Daily 10-5

Clos Pegase Winery
1060 Dunaweal Lane
Calistoga, CA 94515
707-942-4981
www.clospegase.com
Daily 10:30-5:00

Cuvaison Winery
4550 Silverado Trail
Calistoga, CA 94515
707-942-6266
www.cuvaison.com
Daily 10-5

Diamond Creek Vineyards
1500 Diamond Mountain Road
Calistoga, CA 94515
707-942-6926
www.diamondcreekvineyards.com
By appointment only

Domaine Carneros
1240 Duhig Road
Napa, CA 94559
707-257-0101
www.domainecarneros.com
Daily 10:30-6:00

Domaine Chandon
1 California Drive
Yountville, CA 94599
707-944-2280
www.chandonusa.com
Daily 10-6 April-December
Wed-Sun 10-6 January-March

Dominus Estate
2570 Napanook Road
Yountville, CA 94599
707-944-8954
www.dominusestate.com
Not open for tasting or tours

Far Niente
1 Acacia Drive
Oakville, CA 94562
707-944-2861
www.farniente.com
Not open to the public

Franciscan Estates
Franciscan Oakville Estate
1178 Galleron Road
St. Helena, CA 94574
707-967-2130
www.franciscan.com
Daily 10-5 except major holidays

Freemark Abbey Winery
3022 St. Helena Highway North
St. Helena, CA 94574
707-963-9694
www.freemarkabbey.com
Daily 10:00-4:30 October-May
Daily 10-6 June-September

Frog's Leap
8815 Conn Creek Road
Rutherford, CA 94573
707-963-4704
www.frogsleap.com

Grgich Hills Cellar
1829 St. Helena Highway
Rutherford, CA 94573
707-963-2784
www.grgich.com
Daily 9:30-4:30

Hess Collection Winery
4411 Redwood Road
Napa, CA 94558
707-255-1144
www.hesscollection.com
Daily 10-4

Howell Mountain Vineyards
P.O. Box 521
St. Helena, CA 94574
707-967-9676
www.howellmountain.com
By appointment only

Kent Rasmussen Winery
1001 Silverado Trail
St. Helena, CA 94574
707-963-5667
No tasting; retails sales by appointment only

Littorai Wines
St. Helena, CA 94574
707-963-4762
www.littorai.com
Not open to public

Livingston Moffett Winery
1895 Cabernet Lane
St. Helena, CA 94574
707-963-2120
www.livingstonwines.com

Louis M. Martini Winery
254 South St. Helena Highway
St. Helena, CA 94574
707-963-2736
www.louismartini.com
Daily 10:00-4:30

Madonna Estate Mont St. John
5400 Old Sonoma Road
Napa, CA 94559
(707) 255-8864
madonnaestate@madonnaestate.com

Mason Cellars
Napa Wine Co.
7830-40 St. Helena Highway
Oakville, CA 94562
707-944-9159
www.wines@masoncellars.com
Daily 10:30-3:30

Miner Family Winery
Oakville Ranch Vineyards
7850 Silverado Trail
Oakville, CA 94562
707-945-1270
www.minerwines.com
Daily 11–5

Mumm Napa Valley
8445 Silverado Trail
Rutherford, CA 94573
707-942-3434
www.mummnapavalley.com
Daily 10–5

Niebaum-Coppola Estate Winery
1991 St. Helena Highway
Rutherford, CA 94573
707-963-9099
www.niebaum-coppola.com
Daily 10–5

Oakford Vineyards
1575 Oakville Grade
Oakville, CA 94562
707 945 0115
www.oakfordvineyards.com
By appointment only

Opus One
7900 St. Helena Highway
Oakville, CA 94562
707-963-1979
www.opusonewinery.com
Daily 10:30–3:30
Tours by appointment

Peter Michael Winery
12400 Ida Clayton Road
Calistoga, CA 94515
800-354-4459
www.petermichaelwinery.com

Pine Ridge Winery
5901 Silverado Trail
Napa, CA 94558
707-253-7500
www.pineridgewinery.com
Daily 11–5

Quintessa
1501 Silverado Trail
Rutherford, CA 94573
707-963-7111
www.quintessa.com
By appointment only
Tasting at Franciscan Oakville
    Estate

Robert Mondavi Winery
7801 St. Helena Highway
Oakville, CA 94562
707-226-1395
www.robertmondavi.com
Daily 9–4 except major holidays

Rudd Estate
(formerly Girard Winery)
7717 Silverado Trail
Oakville, CA 94562
707-968-9297

Saintsbury
1500 Los Carneros Avenue
Napa, CA 94559
707-252-0592
www.saintsbury.com
By appointment only

Schramsberg Vineyards
1400 Schramsberg Road
Calistoga, CA 94515
707-942-4558
www.schramsberg.com
Daily 10–4 by appointment only

Screaming Eagle Winery &
    Vineyards
7557 Silverado Trail
Napa, CA 94558
707 944 0749
www.screamingeagle.com
Not open to the public

Stag's Leap Wine Cellars
5766 Silverado Trail
Napa, CA 94558
707-944-2020
www.cask23.com
Daily 10:00 4:30
Tours by appointment

Sterling Vineyards
1111 Dunaweal Lane
Calistoga, CA 94515
707-942-3434
www.sterlingvineyards.com
Daily 10:30–4:30

Stony Hill Vineyard
P.O. Box 308
St. Helena, CA 94574
707-963-2636
www.stonyhillvineyard.com

Sutter Home Winery
Trinchero Family Estates
277 St. Helena Highway
St. Helena, CA 94574
707-963-3104
www.sutterhome.com
Daily 10–5

Trefethen Vineyards
1160 Oak Knoll Avenue
Napa, CA 94588
707-255-7700
www.trefethen.com
Daily 10:00–4:30

Truchard Vineyards
3234 Old Sonoma Road
Napa, CA 94559
707-253-7153
www.truchardvineyard.com
By appointment only

V. Sattui Winery
1111 White Lane
St. Helena, CA 94574
707-963-7774
www.vsattui.com
Daily 9–6 daylight savings time
Daily 9–5 daylight standard time

ZD Wines
8383 Silverado Trail
Napa, CA 94558
707-963-5188
www.zdwines.com
Daily 10:00–4:30

Other Attractions

COPIA: The American Center for
    Wine, Food & the Arts
500 First Street
Napa, CA 94559
707-259-1600
www.copia.org

Calistoga Mineral Water
    Company
865 Silverado Trail
Calistoga, CA 94515
707-942-6295
www.calistogawater.com
No tours or tasting but available
    everywhere

Crystal Geyser Water Company
501 Washington Street
Calistoga, CA 94515
707-942-0500
www.crystalgeyserwater.com
No tours or tasting but available
    everywhere

Culinary Institute of America
Greystone Cellars
2555 Main Street
St. Helena, CA 94574
707-963-4503

Napa Valley Wine Auction
899 Adams Street
St. Helena, CA 94574
707-963-3388
www.napavintners.com

Chapter Five

Sonoma Valley

California's Legendary Winemaking Valley

Just as Napa Valley is known by its winemakers and the communities in which they work, so is Sonoma Valley a region of smaller districts and demarcations. It begins in the Carneros district in the south, a patch that straddles the Sonoma and Napa County lines, saturating both with its San Francisco Bay–born fog. The county then stretches up through Sonoma Valley, on to the Alexander Valley and beyond, to the Russian River Valley. Sonoma boasts hundreds of micro-climates and thousands of wine flavors, including many of California's best.

The wine-growing region is a small part of the area of Sonoma County, which itself is more than three times as large as Napa County and ten times the size of Napa Valley. Sonoma County, with its mix of agriculture, viticulture, and suburbia, includes the commuters' artery, Highway 101, leading San Francisco Bay–area workers home to Petaluma, Rohnert Park, and Santa Rosa.

Sonoma has long been viewed as second place to Napa, but this is a result more of slower marketing efforts than of quality. While great wine was being made in Sonoma as early as the 1960s, it was going to market not under the "Sonoma" appellation but merely identified as wine from California's "North Coast." Sonoma was really only discovered in the early 1980s.

One of those who helped propel this discovery was Denver transplant Tom Jordan. The evolving philosophy of the county's wine country suits him perfectly. "Where Napa is almost purely wine," Jordan says over a harvest luncheon with a half-dozen invited guests from Texas and dozens of his vineyard and winery staff, "Sonoma is wine and food. My philosophy is to marry good food with friendly wines."

Jordan, an oil-exploration geologist, has refined his philosophy, and with winemaker Rob Davis, Jordan Vineyard & Winery produces 90,000 cases of Cabernet Sauvignon from his own vineyards in the Alexander Valley near the north end of Sonoma Valley and Chardonnays from several vineyards in the Russian River appellation.

After founding the vineyard and winery in 1972, Jordan began by buying sheep and cattle grazing land and prune and pear orchard country barely twenty miles inland from the Pacific Ocean, still close enough to enjoy cooling morning fogs. His soil had been fed over the centuries by the Russian River. On this land, he planted 275 acres of vines and began building a French-chateau-style winery that makes visitors believe they've been instantly transported to Bordeaux.

An expert in his own field, Jordan turned to another expert for help, André Tchelitscheff, who had retired from Beaulieu Vineyards. Tchelitscheff aided and advised Jordan and present-day winemaker Rob Davis for eighteen years, founding yet another Sonoma legend in the process, the Jordan Cabernets and Chardonnays. In 1976, Jordan's winery was completed, and he made his first bottling, using purchased grapes harvested that same year. By 1978, the estate was producing its own Cabernet grapes, and when the 1976 Cab was released in 1980, it was a hit from the start. Historically, Jordan, Tchelitscheff, and now Davis have blended 75 to 90 percent Jordan Cabernet grapes with 10 to 25 percent Jordan Merlot for a smooth

Previous page:

Buena Vista Carneros

The old winery at Buena Vista still contains ancient-redwood barrels from the time of founder Agoston Haraszthy, although none still contain aging wine. Haraszthy was the first to promote Sonoma as a grape-growing region, beginning with his own 300-acre vineyard in 1860. Sadly, the old building suffered structural damage during recent earthquakes and no longer is open to public tours, although visitors can see the barrels from the open entryway.

Sonoma Selection

From left to right: Buena Vista Carneros 1997 Carneros Cabernet Sauvignon; Buena Vista Carneros 1998 Carneros Chardonnay; Jordan 1997 Sonoma Cabernet Sauvignon; Jordan 1998 Sonoma Chardonnay; Bouchaine 1999 Carneros Chardonnay; Bouchaine 2000 Carneros Rose de Pinot Noir; Bouchaine 1999 Carneros Pinot Noir

fruity flavor. Their Chardonnays are purebloods, made from 100 percent Chardonnay grapes.

Jordan Vineyard & Winery is open year round but tours and tastings are available only by appointment.

Sonoma Legend:
Agoston Haraszthy and Buena Vista

At the other end of the county, and 118 years earlier, Sonoma legend Agoston Haraszthy founded what was probably California's first premium winery, Buena Vista. The winery was built on land and using cuttings Haraszthy acquired from the Spanish territorial governor, General Mariano Vallejo. The Governor had only a 300-square-foot vineyard, but Haraszthy had larger ambitions. His first vineyard, in place by 1860, covered 300 acres; two years later it was 400 acres. It was planted, he boasted, with 280 varieties of grapes. According to Buena Vista records, Haraszthy had invested a fortune for the time. It cost him $50 per acre to plant and set up his vineyards; adjusted for today's prices, it cost about $1,200 per acre, an incredible bargain for any vineyard anywhere today. Haraszthy claimed it was California's largest—and it may actually have been as it was forty acres larger than his contemporary H. W. Osborne's in Napa.

By the late 1870s, Haraszthy's vineyards were being run by his sons, Arpad and Attila. Then Phylloxera root louse devastated the plants, and the vineyard fell into disuse until the 1940s. In 1979, the Moller-Racke family and A. Racke GmbH of Oberwesel, Germany, acquired the winery and began efforts to bring it back to its first glory. Now, with 935 planted acres on the 1,360-acre farm in Carneros, Buena Vista is producing 135,000 cases of a variety of wines.

Buena Vista Winery is open for tours and tastings at its Haraszthy Cellars in Sonoma.

The Carneros District:
Where Napa and Sonoma Meet

The Carneros district is a home away from home to many of the greatest winemakers of Sonoma and Napa who have acreage there. The quality of the Carneros *terroir* is the only thing the rival counties of Napa and Sonoma agree

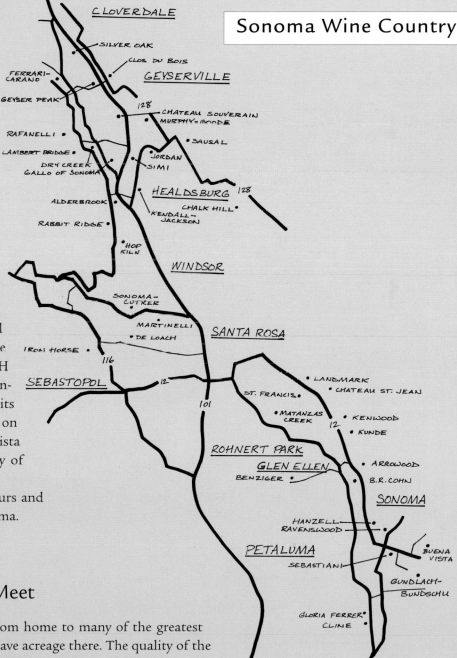

on: Vineyards there produce great grapes. Sonoma champagne-makers Domaine Chandon has 780 acres and Gloria Ferrer has 340, while Napa's Robert Mondavi and Clos Pegase has 365 and Beaulieu has 345. At the smaller end of the investment scale, Napa's ZD has 28 acres and Casa Carneros has just 7.

Carneros was designated a distinct viticultural area by the U.S. Department of Agriculture in 1983. *Carneros* means "ram" or "sheep" in Spanish, and indeed the area was rangeland before the mid-nineteenth century when the first of the winemakers recognized the quality of the soil and the value of San Francisco Bay's cooling breezes and dense fog.

Sonoma County Wineries

The history of Sonoma County is farming. That story began with Russian fur trappers who first moved into the area around 1812, about a dozen years before the Spanish missionaries arrived. Some fifty years later, Italian immigrants began to reach the northern edges of the area. Each group brought with it the fruits, vegetables, and livestock of its heritage and, over time, came to realize the value of this land and its climate for raising wine grapes.

Today, many great wines come from Sonoma. Wineries in Cloverdale include Fritz Winery.

In Fulton, visit Williams Selyem Winery.

Wineries in Geyserville include Chateau Souverain Winery (plan to arrive at meal time to enjoy their excellent café), Geyser Peak Winery, Murphy-Goode Winery, and Silver Oak Cellars.

Above and facing page:
Jordan Vineyard & Winery
A harvest supervisor keeps count as each picker dumps his or her forty-pound tub of Cabernet Sauvignon grapes into one of Jordan's gondolas. Picking begins at first light, often in 45- or 50-degree temperatures. The work-day ends at 3 p.m., interrupted by a few rest breaks and lunch. Most pickers at Jordan are year-round employees who fill other jobs during the rest of the year.

In Glen Ellen, there are Arrowood Vineyards & Winery, Benziger Family Winery, and B. R. Cohn Winery.

The Healdsburg area is home to numerous wineries, including Alderbrook Winery, Chalk Hill Estate, Clos du Bois Wines, Dry Creek Vineyard, Gary Farrell Winery, Ferrari-Carano Winery, Hop Kiln Winery, Kendall-Jackson Winery, Lambert-Bridge Winery, Rabbit Ridge Winery, Rafanelli Winery, Rochiolli Vineyards, Sausal Winery, Seghisio Family Vineyards, and Simi Winery.

In Kenwood, visit Chateau St. Jean, Kenwood Vineyards, Kunde Estate Winery, Landmark Vineyards, and St. Francis Winery.

Wineries in Santa Rosa include Matanzas Creek Winery.

To the west in the Russian River region are Tom Dehlinger's noted Dehlinger Winery, Iron Horse Vineyards, and Kistler Vineyards.

In the city of Sonoma, there is Gundlach-Bundschu Winery, Hanzell Vineyards, MacRostie Winery, Ravenswood Winery, and Sebastiani Sonoma Cask Cellars.

In Windsor, visit Martinelli Winery and Sonoma-Cutrer Vineyards.

Finally, toward the Sonoma coast is Marcassin Vineyards run by Helen Turley, one of California's most talented winemakers.

Sonoma Winery Architecture

For architectural enthusiasts, Sonoma also has much to offer, beginning with Haraszthy's old Buena Vista cellars and the replica of his villa at Bartholemew Memorial Park. French in name, Chateau St. Jean is also northern French in design; here, owner Gloria Ferrer brings her Catalonian influence to Sonoma.

Sebastiani Vineyards is located only two blocks from California's most northern mission, San Francisco de Solano at Sonoma. Sebastiani dates from 1904, although its vineyards are those of the mission, replanted in 1824. Sebastiani is well worth a visit to see its barrel room, with the largest collection of hand-carved barrel caps in the world, created within the past thirty-five years by Sebastiani family friend Earle Brown.

Chateau Souverain is another imposing structure whose architecture cleverly assimilates French chateau style with the structural shape of hop-drying kilns. Hops were a significant crop of Sonoma County beginning around 1900 after Phylloxera wiped out vineyards in the 1870s and 1880s. A tenacious climbing plant, hops are used in beer brewing as a natural preservative, giving beers their uniquely bitter tastes. The same motif identifies Hop Kiln Winery in Healdsburg, but the three towers incorporated into the winery were drying kilns. Hop Kiln's tasting room and tours of the buildings and winemaking facilities are available by appointment only.

Still another wonderful building is the Iron Horse Vineyards residence. Though it's not open for tours, it is a fine example of a one-hundred-year-old Carpenter Gothic farmhouse.

Jordan Vineyard & Winery
Reminiscent in many ways of France's wine country, Jordan's formal and informal gardens offer visitors gorgeous vistas and comfortable shady seating on warm summer days. The winery occupies about 1,200 acres but only 275 are planted in Cabernet Sauvignon grapes and olive trees, leaving the rest for casual walks and peaceful contemplation. While wine tastings and tours at Jordan are done only by appointments, the grounds are open to the public to enjoy, and the French Chateau-style architecture is a treat to the eye. Just outside the main visitor's entrance a small courtyard surrounds a bronze sculpture of Bacchus, the Greek god of wine.

Sonoma

The Sonoma City Hall sits at the center of the city's Plaza. A large park surrounds the structure that is rimmed with wine shops and other merchants and restaurants. The Plaza is anchored on the north by the centuries-old Sonoma Mission and the adobe dwellings for the Franciscan friars and their Native American neophytes.

Sonoma

Sonoma builder and winery owner Steve Ledson has developed a small community of Victorian and Craftsman homes just to the east of Sonoma's city Plaza, along East Napa Street. The area, called Armstrong Estates, surrounds the winery owner's own Victorian at the center. The community features large lots and lush gardens.

Buena Vista Carneros

A seldom-used dining room inside the old winery at Buena Vista still yields a few treasures to an inquisitive eye. Bottles of the 1857–1997 140-year Celebration wine suggest one of the last parties held in the building. Buena Vista now makes its wines at a state-of-the-art facility several miles south of the historic winery.

Healdsburg

Downtown Healdsburg is a small village surrounding a park, or plaza, similar to Sonoma's layout. More of Healdsburg's retail and commercial development, including new hotels and fine restaurants and shops, is taking place along Healdsburg Avenue as it parallels U.S. Highway 101.

Ferrari-Carano Winery
The Italianate Villa Fiore at Ferrari-Carano opened in 1994 as the winery's hospitality center. With eighteen vineyards in Alexander Valley, Russian River Valley, Dry Creek Valley, and the Carneros district, Ferrari-Carano wines represents most of the famous Sonoma winemaking regions.

The Art of the Wine Label: Information and Inspiration

In the early days, the labels affixed to wine bottles were straightforward and simple. They provided the name, vintage, and appellation of a wine, and little more. In the past two decades, however, label design has become as much an art form as the making of the finest wine. It is no longer enough to be informational; labels must now be inspirational. Wine labels can cost wineries dearly—as much as two dollars apiece for five- or six-color printing, embossing, die-cutting, and gold- or silver-foiling. Still, few winemakers question their value. The label is the first taste one gets of the wine inside.

Bonny Doon Vineyard
A stylish die-cut label adorns Bonny Doon's Pacific Rim Dry Riesling.

Clos Pegase
Clos Pegase's label exudes style and class.

Bonny Doon Vineyard
Bonny Doon's Randall Grahm has a self-professed fascination with "utterly unexpected" wines blending Rhône—especially Châteauneuf du Pape wines—and Italian flavors, and his daring wine labels mirror his wine's image.

Above:
Bonny Doon Vineyard
With artwork by Hunter S. Thompson's old ally Ralph Steadman, the label for Bonny Doon's Cardinal Zin is stunning and shocking.

Left:
Opus One
Understated elegance is the trademark of Robert Mondavi and Baron Philippe de Rothschild's Opus One label.

Chateau St. Jean Winery

The chateau at Chateau St. Jean Winery was built in 1920 as a family summer home for the Goff family of Michigan. The winery was founded in 1973, and the chateau's 250 acres were planted with vineyards. Chateau St. Jean sits in The Valley of the Moon, named by Indians who were enchanted by the moon that passed seven times over the mountain peaks as it rose in the sky.

Sonoma Valley's Best Wines and Wineries

Cabernet Sauvignons

Arrowood Reserve Speciale
Ferrari-Carano
Geyser Peak Estate Reserve
Kenwood

Chardonnays

Arrowood Reserve
Ferrari-Carano Reserve
Jordan
Kendall-Jackson's JSJ Signature
    Series Chardonnays
Kistler Vineyards
Marcassin
Martinelli
Peter Michael
Rabbit Ridge Chardonnays
Rochioli

Merlots

Arrowood Reserve Speciale
Chateau Souverain
Ferrari-Carano
Gary Farrell Ladi's Vineyard
Ravenswood
Simi

Pinot Noirs

Dehlinger
Kistler
Rochioli Reserve

Sparkling Wines

Iron Horse

Syrahs

Arrowood
Dehlinger Estate
Ridge Petite Sirah

Zinfandels

De Loach OFS
Gallo of Sonoma
Rafanelli
Ravenswood
Ridge Vineyards

Chateau Souverain Winery

Chateau Souverain founder J. Leland "Lee" Stewart was one of the visionary trendsetters of California winemaking. He began harvesting wine grapes at his Howell Mountain property in Napa Valley in 1944 and was soon winning silver medals at the California State Fair for his Zinfandel and Pinot Noir. Stewart was among the first in California to concentrate on single-varietal wines. He introduced Petite Sirah as a varietal and made style-defining Zinfandels and Johannisberg Rieslings. His winery was named "Souverain" from the French word for "sovereign" or "supreme."

Sonoma County Winery and Vineyard Resources

Alderbrook Winery
2306 Magnolia Drive
Healdsburg, CA 95448
707-433-9154
www.alderbrook.com
Daily 10-5
Tours by appointment

Arrowood Vineyards & Winery
14347 Sonoma Highway
Glen Ellen, CA 95442
707-938-5170
www.arrowoodvineyards.com
Daily 10:00-4:30

B. R. Cohn Winery
15000 Sonoma Highway
Glen Ellen, CA 95442
707-938-4064
www.brcohnwinery.com
Daily 10-5

Benziger Family Winery
1883 London Ranch Road
Glen Ellen, CA 95442
707-935-3000
www.benziger.com
Daily 10-5

Buena Vista Carneros
18000 Old Winery Road
Sonoma, CA 95476
707-938-1266
www.buenavistawinery.com
Daily 10-5

Chalk Hill Estate
10300 Chalk Hill Road
Healdsburg, CA 95448
707-838-4306
www.chalkhill.com
By appointment only

Chateau Souverain Winery &
    Café
400 Souverain Road
Geyserville, CA 95441
707-433-8281
www.chateausouverain.com
Daily 10-5

Chateau St. Jean Winery
8555 Sonoma Highway
Kenwood, CA 95452
707-833-4134
www.chateaustjean.com
Daily 10-4

Cline Cellars
24737 Highway 121
Sonoma, CA 95476
707-935-4310
www.clinecellars.com

Clos du Bois Wines
19410 Geyserville Avenue
Geyserville, CA 95441
707-857-3100
www.closdubois.com
Daily 10:00-4:30

De Loach Vineyards
1791 Olivet Road
Santa Rosa, CA 95401
707-526-9111
www.deloachvineyards.com
Daily 10:00-4:30

Dry Creek Vineyard
3770 Lambert Bridge Road
Healdsburg, CA 95448
707-433-1000
www.drycreekvineyard.com
Daily 10:30-4:30 except major
    holidays

Ferrari-Carano Winery
8761 Dry Creek Road
Healdsburg, CA 95448
707-433-6700
www.ferrari-carano.com
Daily 10-5

Fritz Winery
24691 Dutcher Creek Road
Cloverdale, CA 95425
707-894-3389
www.fritzwinery.com
Daily 11-4:30

Gallo of Sonoma Winery
3387 Dry Creek Road
Healdsburg, CA 95448
www.gallosonoma.com
Not open for tasting or tours

Gary Farrell Winery
10701 Westside Road
Healdsburg, CA 95448
707-473-2900
www.garyfarrell.com
Thu-Sun by appointment only

Geyser Peak Winery
22281 Chianti Road
Geyserville, CA 95441
707-857-9463
www.geyserpeakwinery.com
Daily 10-5

Gloria Ferrer Champagne Caves
23555 Highway 121
Sonoma, CA 95476
707-933-1917
www.gloriaferrer.com
Daily 10:30-5:15

Gundlach-Bundschu Winery
2000 Denmark Street
Sonoma, CA 95476
707-938-5277
www.gunbun.com
Daily 11:00-4:30

Hanzell Vineyards
18596 Lomita Avenue
Sonoma, CA 95476
707-996-3860
www.hanzell.com
Tues and Fri by appointment
    only

Hop Kiln Winery
6050 Westside Road
Healdsburg, CA 95448
707-433-6491
www.hopkilnwinery.com
Daily 10-5

Iron Horse Vineyards
9786 Ross Station Road
Sebastopol, CA 95472
707-887-1507
www.ironhorsevineyards.com
Daily 10:00-3:30

Jordan Vineyard & Winery
1474 Alexander Valley Road
P.O. Box 878
Healdsburg, CA 95448
707-431-5250
www.jordanvineyard.citysearch.com
By appointment only

Kendall-Jackson Wine Estates
5007 Fulton Road
Fulton, CA 95403
707-571-8100
www.kj.com
Daily 10-5

Kenwood Vineyards
9592 Sonoma Highway (12)
Kenwood, CA 95452
707-833-5891
www.kenwoodvineyards.com
Daily 10:00-4:30

Kistler Vineyards
Sebastopol, CA 95472
707-823-5603
blewis@kistlerwine.com
Not open to the public

Kunde Estate Winery
10155 Sonoma Highway (12)
Kenwood, CA 95452
707-833-5501
www.kunde.com
Daily 10:30-4:30 summer
Daily 10:30-4 winter

Lambert Bridge Winery
4085 West Dry Creek Road
Healdsburg, CA 95448
707-431-9600
www.lambertbridge.com
Daily 10:30-4:30

Landmark Vineyards
101 Adobe Canyon Road
Kenwood, CA 95452
707-833-0053
www.landmarkwine.com
Daily 10:00-4:30

Laurel Glen Vineyard
Glen Ellen, CA 95442
707-526-3914
www.laurelglen.com
Not open to public

MacRostie Winery
P.O. Box 340
Sonoma, CA 95476
707-996-4480
www.macrostiewinery.com
By appointment only

Martinelli Winery
3360 River Road
Windsor, CA 95492
707-525-0570
www.martinelliwinery.com
Daily 10-5

Matanzas Creek Winery
6097 Bennett Valley Road
Santa Rosa, CA 95404
707-528-6464
www.matanzascreek.com
Daily 10:00–4:30

Mueller Winery
Healdsburg, CA 95448
707-837-7399
www.muellerwine.com
Not open to the public

Murphy-Goode Winery
4001 Highway 128
Geyserville, CA 95441
707-431-7644
www.murphygoodewinery.com
Daily 10:30–4:30

Rabbit Ridge Winery
3291 Westside Road
Healdsburg, CA 95448
707-431-7128
www.rabbitridgewinery.com
Daily 11–5

Rafanelli Winery
4685 West Dry Creek Road
Healdsburg, CA 95448
707-433-1385
By appointment only

Ravenswood Winery
18701 Gehricke Road
Sonoma, CA 95476
707-933-2332
www.ravenswood-wine.com
Daily 10:00–4:30

Rochioli Winery
6182 Westside Road
Healdsburg, CA 95448
707-433-2305
By appointment only

Sausal Winery
7370 Highway 128
Healdsburg, CA 95448
707-433-2285
www.sausalwinery.com
Daily 10–4 except major holidays

Sebastiani Vineyards
389 Fourth Street East
Sonoma, CA 95476
707-938-5532
www.sebastiani.com
Daily 10–5

Seghesio Family Vineyards
14730 Grove Street
Healdsburg, CA 95448
707-433-3579
www.seghesio.com
Daily 10:00–4:30 except major
    holidays

Silver Oak Cellars
24625 Chianti Road
Geyserville, CA 95441
707-857-3562
www.silveroak.com
Daily 9–4, closed Sun

Simi Winery
16275 Healdsburg Avenue
Healdsburg, CA 95448
707-433-6981
www.simiwinery.com
Daily 10–5

Sonoma-Cutrer Vineyards
4401 Slusser Road
Windsor, CA 95492
707-528-1181
www.sonomacutrer.com
By appointment only

St. Francis Winery
100 Pythian Road
Santa Rosa, CA 95409
707-833-4666
www.stfranciswine.com
Daily 10–5

Stonestreet Winery
7111 Highway 128
Healdsburg, CA 95448
707-433-9463
www.stonestreetwines.com
Not open to the public

Williams Selyem Winery
6575 Westside Road
Healdsburg, CA 95448
707-433-6425
www.williams-selyem.com
Tours December–June only

Chapter Six

Mendocino County and Lake County

The North Country Wineries

Timber is still the largest income producer in Mendocino County, although grape growing, winemaking, and related tourism are the largest industry now in this vast region despite the fact that nearly all of it is limited to the eastern half of the county.

The winemaking history in this county parallels what occurred in Napa and Sonoma with the earliest vines planted by Gold Rush settlers in the 1850s. These Europeans planted grapes on the hillsides and ridges, looking for slightly cooler temperatures and adequate rainwater runoff. Mendocino's first winery was founded in 1879 by Louis Finne, near Hopland. By 1900, there were some 3,000 acres of wine grapes growing, although lack of good roads and any railway made transporting bottled or barreled wines difficult until after Prohibition ended in 1933.

Ironically, Adolph Parducci founded one of Mendocino's best-known and most productive wineries in 1932, two years before the individual states ratified Prohibition's repeal. A tour of the winery offers many enjoyable stories on the legitimate and not-so-legitimate wine industry from 1919 to 1933.

Mendocino's wines have evolved and changed with the times. After Prohibition's demise, many of the county's winemakers produced mostly jug wines until the 1960s, when several makers began to try new varieties. For the most part, Mendocino County offers growers a short but hot growing season.

The far west edge of the county along the Pacific shore offers less-hospitable growing conditions, but one vineyard and winery is trying its luck here and it is worth a visit, as if one needed an excuse to drive this most-spectacular stretch of California's coastline. With daytime high temperatures averaging only in the 60s and with frequent coastal fog and on-shore breezes, these are not ideal grape-growing conditions. But less than ten miles north of the city of Fort Bragg, Pacific Star Winery has planted its vines on wind-whipped bluffs in sight of the coast's rocks and ocean breakers. However, the climate there is hard on grape vines, and so Pacific Star currently makes its wines from grapes grown further inland.

Marrying Wine and Food

If Napa's Robert Mondavi is encouraging the appreciation of food with wine in the county's new American Center for Wine, Food and the Arts, and Sonoma County boasts that its reason for existing is to marry food and wine, then Mendocino County is here to prove the marriage will work.

Barney Fetzer, a lumber company executive, bought his first ranch in 1958 north of Ukiah, in Redwood Valley. He raised grapes mostly for the home-winemaking markets until 1968 when he marketed his first wines. By the time he died in 1981, ten of his eleven children were involved in what had become the new family business: grape growing and winemaking. They acquired the Valley Oaks ranch in Hopland, where the tasting room and visitor center are located now. After another decade, the family built the winery from a 200,000-case-per-year producer to 2.2 million in 1992. The winery was sold to Kentucky liquor conglomerate Brown-Forman, although the family held onto its vineyards. Fetzer is a huge producer, and its red-wine barrel room contains 45,000 barrels, an astonishing sight. Fetzer is currently the county's largest winemaker and the nation's sixth largest, producing nearly 3 million cases annually. Still, the company also

Mendocino Selection
Left to right: Fetzer Vineyard 1999 Eagle Peak California Merlot; Fetzer Vineyard 2000 Echo Ridge California Sauvignon Blanc; Husch 1998 Mendocino Cabernet Sauvignon; Frey California Red Table Wine; Guenoc 1998 Genevieve Magoon-Langtry Guenoc Valley Chardonnay

produces some true boutique varieties with outputs in the hundreds of cases. These limited varietals alone make the visit worthwhile.

Within the fifty-acre vineyard surrounding Fetzer's Valley Oak facility is a five-acre vegetable and fruit garden that is the foundation of Fetzer's fascination with organically grown fresh food. This is a facility that has not only four winemakers—lead by Dennis Martin—but also a culinary director, John Ash. Visitors can picnic on Fetzer's grounds from food raised entirely in Fetzer's gardens.

Organic Vineyards and Wineries

In recent years, Fetzer has been a leader in growing its grapes organically, a farming style now popular in Mendocino with as much as half of the grape growers. Fetzer's 357 acres of vineyards in Mendocino County are all farmed without pesticides or herbicides.

Lolonis Vineyards in Redwood Valley has been farming without chemicals for forty-five years, marking it as the first organic grape grower in the county, if not the state. The practice serves the small winery well; its wines are well regarded and continually sell out. Lolonis is open only by appointment but it's worth the visit.

Another all-organic winemaker is Frey Vineyards in Redwood Valley. Founded in 1980, it lays claim to the title of America's most complete organic operation. What isn't organic at Frey often is recycled. Most of the building materials for the winery came from an older winery in Ukiah. All the fermentation tanks were recycled from other wineries. And the wines are highly regarded, with the grapes for their Sauvignon Blanc, Chardonnay, and Cabernet Sauvignon originating in their own vineyards. Frey is open by appointment only.

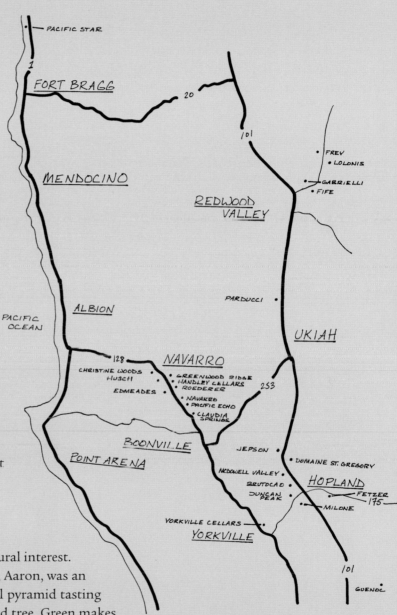

Mendocino County Wineries

Greenwood Ridge Vineyards in Philo is of architectural interest. Winery owner and winemaker Allan Green's father, Aaron, was an associate of Frank Lloyd Wright, and the octagonal pyramid tasting room was built from the lumber of a single redwood tree. Green makes a notable Merlot and Cabernet Sauvignon, among other varieties.

Handley Cellars in Philo also integrates food and wine during its first-weekend-of-the-month Culinary Adventures, with food coming from its own gardens, similar to Fetzer. The winery is open daily but tours are offered by appointment only.

Jepson Vineyards, Winery & Distillery in Ukiah offers something for everyone, and its Sauvignon Blanc is well regarded. The property originally was home to the modern William Baccala Estate winery, founded in 1982. In 1985, Robert Jepson acquired the 106-acre vineyards and the winery with its elegant copper evaporative-condensing alembic-type distilling apparatus still used for making Jepson's brandy.

While touring Mendocino's wineries, do not miss Brutocao Cellars & Vineyards with its tasting rooms in Philo and Hopland. Be sure to visit Duncan Peak Vineyards, McDowell Valley Vineyards, Milano Family Winery, Domaine Saint Gregory, Monte Volpe Vineyards, and Fetzer Vineyards in Hopland. In Redwood Valley, there are Elizabeth Vineyards, Fife Vineyards, Frey Vineyards, Gabrielli Winery, and Lolonis Winery. In Yorkville on Highway 128, visit Yorkville Cellars. If you arrive in the right season, some 500 blooming roses will welcome you.

Don't forget Ukiah with Hidden Cellars (acquired by Parducci in 1999), Jepson Vineyards, Parducci Wine Estates, and notably, the tiny Whaler Cellars with its excellent limited release Zinfandels.

Several smaller Mendocino winemakers rely on one outlet for their tasting and retail sales. Claudia Springs Winery, Lonetree Winery, and Eaglepoint Ranch Winery, each located in Philo, have no tasting room but their fine wines can be tasted and purchased at Mendocino Specialty Vineyards in Boonville.

Lastly, in Philo, be sure to visit Edmeades Winery, Esterlina Vineyards & Winery (formerly Pepperwood Springs and now with its own tasting room), Greenwood Ridge Vineyards, Handley Cellars, Husch Vineyards, Lazy Creek Vineyards, Pacific Echo Cellars, Roederer Estate, Christine Woods Winery, and especially Navarro Vineyards.

Ted Bennett and Deborah Cahn founded Navarro in 1974. They started slowly with only Gewürztraminer but now offer a range including a Cabernet, Pinot Noir, Chardonnay, and three varieties of Riesling. They are bold in refusing to sell any compromises, and their tough standards have rewarded them with loyal customers and high regard. Most of their output of about 25,000 cases is sold through mail order or out of the tasting room. Don't miss these wines or the tasting room overlooking their beautiful vineyards.

Finally, there is Jed Steele's Steele Winery, maker of a superlative Chardonnay.

Lake County Wineries

To the east of Mendocino County is Lake County, a more recent entry in winemaking in the state, although grape growers have raised excellent varietals in the county for decades. So far, only a few wineries call Lake County home. Less than twenty miles over the pass from Calistoga at the northern end of Napa County is the Quenoc district's Middletown with its Quenoc Winery and Langtry Estates Winery.

The drive to Middletown will take you past several large, lovely vineyards. Up and over another pass leads you to Kelseyville and the large Clear Lake for which the county is named. While there, stop in and taste the medal-winning wines at Wildhurst Vineyard on Main Street.

Above and facing page:

Mendocino

The village of Mendocino often reminds many visitors more of Cape Cod, Massachusetts, than of coastal California. Houses large and small used to support their own water tanks on towers, and many structures still have the towers if not the tanks looming above them.

Point Cabrillo lighthouse
Point Cabrillo lighthouse sits not quite four miles north of the village of Mendocino. A group of local lighthouse volunteers recently completed renovating the building and its beautiful Fresnel lens. They open it to daytime visitors willing to make a short hike.

Above and top right:

Fetzer Vineyards

Mendocino County is home to the state's most ecologically conscious wineries and vineyards. More growers here raise grapes organically without pesticides or herbicides. Fetzer goes further, using solar power as the primary energy source for its administrative center and other buildings at its North Coast Winery north of its Valley Oaks Vineyard. The visitor center offers Fetzer's wines and a deli that makes abundant use of fruit and vegetables grown nearby. The Valley Oaks facility offers a cooking school, and a shaded picnic pergola invites leisurely lunches. Wine writers have rhapsodized about spending a day at Fetzer, and now with Fetzer's Bed & Breakfast, it's possible to spend a night or more as well. Rooms are elegant, and patio doors open right onto rows of vines. Or guests can stay in the Haas House, a fully restored century-old farmhouse surrounded by graceful oak trees.

Left:

Redwood Valley

Logging and lumber milling is still the primary income source for Mendocino County. But scenes like this in Redwood Valley, where Burgess Lumber is surrounded by vineyards, hint at the future—especially in a state that is friendly to grape growers and winemakers and noticeably less so to logging interests.

Above:

Haiku Vineyards

People in Mendocino, especially near Ukiah, speak softly about their county's beauty. They mention in a whisper that Eastside Road, shown here passing Haiku Vineyards, is like Napa's Silverado Trail in the early 1980s— beautiful and scarcely traveled.

Facing page:

Buich Vineyards

In Mendocino's Redwood Valley, Buich Vineyards snugs right up against the trees along Reeves Canyon Road. Vineyards and wineries represent a small amount of the total acreage of Mendocino County, yet winemaking has become its largest industry.

Above:

Yorkville Cellars

Three main highways serve as arteries through Mendocino County, and each takes visitors past wineries and restaurants. California Highway 128 cuts north-west from U.S. 101 and takes travelers past Yorkville Cellars, where 500 rose bushes line the driveway, holding back Merlot vines planted by owners Edward and Debbie Wallo.

Top and middle right:

Navarro Vineyards

There are many reasons to journey to Mendocino County—not just less traffic and a more agreeable pace to wine-country touring. Many wineries sell some of their output exclusively at the winery. Navarro Vineyards' owners Ted Bennett and Deborah Cahn keep a portion of their output only for those who visit or stopped by in the past and have joined Navarro's mailing list. Navarro's size allows it to produce small amounts of specific varieties, lately bottling unfiltered and filtered wines of the same vintage and variety, providing customers discriminating taste experiences. A picnic at Navarro allows visitors to gaze over the Chardonnay vines.

Bottom right:

Whaler Cellars

Whaler Cellars is celebrated among knowledgeable wine drinkers for its Zinfandels, yet it sells most of its fruit to larger winemakers in the state. Russ and Anne Nyborg hold some back for their own label, and visitors usually end up tasting wines in the living room overlooking the beautiful vineyard.

Greenwood Ridge Vineyards

Greenwood Ridge owner Allan Green is a renaissance man, part-time artist and designer, some-time radio disc jockey, and winemaker. His vineyard, at 1,200-foot elevation in the Anderson Valley, is just six miles from the Pacific Ocean, providing cooling breezes for his grapes.

Weathered barns

Along California Highway 128, heading from U.S. 101 out to the Pacific Coast, one gets glimpses of the agricultural heritage of Mendocino County and California. This cluster of weathered barns is just east of the village of Navarro.

Navarro

Sunset rakes across California Highway 128 through the village of Navarro as a ranch truck passes Greenwood Ridge. Roads that twist and turn along stream beds and cattle paths dictate a slower pace. As a visitor, allow plenty of time not only to travel but also to enjoy the wild beauty of the county.

Above:

Parducci Wine Estates

Italian immigrant Adolph Parducci settled in the Mendocino area as it reminded him of his native Tuscany. Here, he bought his first vineyard in 1921 and founded one of Mendocino's first wineries in 1932.

Facing page:

Backroads

Some of the backroads of Mendocino County are not suitable for those in a hurry. They meander and swerve, following ancient streams and old cow paths. Set a reasonable pace, and allow a second or third day to visit additional Mendocino wineries throughout this vast and beautiful county.

Mendocino County Winery and Vineyard Resources

Brutocao Cellars & Vineyards
7000 Highway 128
Philo, CA 95466
707-895-2152
Daily 10–5
and
13500 South Highway 101
Hopland, CA 95449
707-744-1664
www.brutocaocellars.com
Daily 10–5

Christine Woods Winery
3155 Highway 128
Philo, CA 95466
707-895-2115
www.christinewoods.com
Daily 11–5

Claudia Springs Winery
Philo, CA 95466
707-895-3926
www.claudiasprings.com
Not open to public
Tasting at Mendocino Specialty
    Vineyards

Domaine Saint Gregory
Tasting Room: 13251 South
    Highway 101 Suite 3
Hopland, CA 95449
707-744-8466
Daily 10–5
Winery: 1170 Bel Arbres Road
Redwood Valley, CA 95470
707-485-9463
www.domainesaintgregory.com
Tours and tasting by appoint-
    ment only

Duncan Peak Vineyards
Box 358
Hopland, CA 95449
707-283-3632
www.duncanpeak.com
By appointment only

Edmeades Winery
5500 Highway 128
Philo, CA 90466
707-895-3232
www.edmeades.com
By appointment only

Elizabeth Vineyards
8591 Colony Drive
Redwood Valley, CA 95470
707-485-9009
By appointment only

Esterlina Vineyards & Winery
(formerly Pepperwood Springs)
1200 Holmes Ranch Road
Philo, CA 95466
www.esterlina.com
707-895-2920
Mon–Thur 11–4
Fri–Sun 11–5

Fetzer Vineyards
13601 East Side Road
Hopland, CA 95449
707-744-1250
www.fetzervineyards.com
Daily 9–5

Fife Vineyards
3620 Road B
Redwood Valley, CA 95470
707-485-0323
www.fifevineyards.com
Daily 10–5

Frey Vineyards
14000 Tomki Road
Redwood Valley, CA 95470
707-485-5177
www.freywine.com
By appointment only

Gabrielli Winery
10950 West Road
Redwood Valley, CA 95470
707-485-1221
www.gabrielliwinery.com
Mon–Fri 10–5
Weekends, holidays, and tours by
    appointment

Greenwood Ridge Vineyards
5501 Highway 128
Philo, CA 95466
707-895-2002
www.greenwoodridge.com
Daily 10–6 daylight savings time
Daily 10–5 daylight standard
    time

Handley Cellars
3151 Highway 128
Philo, CA 95466
707-895-3876
800-733-3151
www.handleycellars.com
Daily 11–6 Memorial Day to
    Labor Day
Daily 11–5 Labor Day to
    Memorial Day

Husch Vineyards
4400 Highway 128
Philo, CA 95466
707-895-3216
www.huschvineyards.com
Daily 10–5

Jepson Vineyards, Winery &
    Distillery
10400 Highway 101
Ukiah, CA 95482
707-468-8936
www.jepsonwine.com
Daily 10–5

Lazy Creek Vineyards
47410 Highway 128
Philo, CA 95466
707-895-3623
By appointment only

Lolonis Winery
1905 Road D
Redwood Valley, CA 95470
925-938-8066
www.lolonis.com
By appointment only

Lonetree Winery
Eaglepoint Ranch
Philo, CA 95466
707-463-0635
www.lonetreewine.com
Not open to public
Tasting at Mendocino Specialty
    Vineyards

McDowell Valley Vineyards
13380 South Highway 101
Hopland, CA 95449
707-744-8911
www.mcdowellsyrah.com
Daily 10–5
11–4 November to April

Mendocino Specialty Vineyards
17810 A Farrer Lane
Boonville, CA 95415
707-895-3993
Daily 10–6

Milone Family Winery
14594 South Highway 101
Hopland, CA 95449
707-744-1396
www.milonefamilywinery.com
Daily 10–5

Navarro Vineyards
5601 Highway 128
Philo, CA 95466
707-895-3686
www.navarrowine.com
Daily 10–6 daylight savings time
Daily 10–5 daylight standard
    time

Pacific Echo Cellars
8501 Highway 128
Philo, CA 95466
707-895-2065
www.pacific-echo.com
Daily 11–5

Pacific Star Winery
33000 North Highway 1
Fort Bragg, CA 95437
707-964-1155
www.pacificstarwinery.com
Daily 11–5 April–November
Weekends December–April or by
    appointment

Parducci Wine Estates
501 Parducci Road
Ukiah, CA 95482
707-462-9463
www.parducci.com
Mon–Sat 10–5
Sun 10–4

Roederer Estate
4501 Highway 128
Philo, CA 95466
707-895-2288
www.roederer-estate.com
Daily 11–5

Whaler Vineyard
6200 Eastside Rd
Ukiah, CA 95482
707-462-6355
www.wineresearch.com
By appointment only

Yorkville Cellars
Milemarker 40.4
Highway 128
Yorkville, CA 95494
707-894-9177
www.yorkvillecellars.com
Daily 11–6 daylight savings time
Thur–Mon 11–5 daylight
    standard time

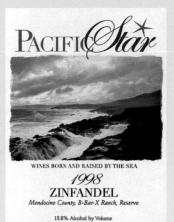

Mendocino County and Lake County's Best Wine and Wineries

Brutocao Sauvignon Blancs
Brutocao Zinfandels
Edmeades Sirahs
Edmeades Zinfandels
Frey Zinfandels
Guenoc Zinfandels
Handley Cellars Alchemy White Wines
Kendall-Jackson Camelot Vineyard
   Chardonnays
Navarro Sauvignon Blancs
Parducci Cabernet Sauvignons
Parducci Merlots
Roederer Sparkling Wines
Steele Chardonnays
Whaler Zinfandels

Lake County Winery and Vineyard Resources

Guenoc & Langtry Estates Vineyards & Winery
21000 Butts Canyon Road
Middletown, CA 95461
707-987-2385
www.guenoc.com
Daily 11:30–5:00

Wildhurst Vineyard
3855 Main Street
Kelseyville, CA 95451
707-279-4302
www.wildhurst.com
Daily 10–5

Chapter Seven

Around San Francisco Bay

Wineries in the Shadows of the Cities

These days it's much easier to conceive of the Bay area as a place to drink wine than to make it. By geographical description, the Bay area extends from Marin County north of the Golden Gate, east past Napa and Sonoma, and south to include Contra Costa, Alameda, Santa Clara, San Mateo, and finally Santa Cruz Counties. It is one of the United States's most densely populated urban regions, incorporating San Francisco, Oakland, San Jose, and Santa Cruz among hundreds of others cities. Historically, before real estate development swallowed every square foot, the region was home to much winemaking, and it still contains some vineyards and a few wineries. But they're elusive.

Marin County Vineyards and Wineries

There are several vineyards in Marin that you might happen across by accident, but nearly all of them sell their grapes to winemakers out of the county, much of it going to wineries in Napa and Sonoma. One exception is Kalin Cellars in Novato where the opposite is true. Kalin imports grapes from Sonoma and the Livermore area to make its Chardonnay and Pinot Noir. Output is around 7,000 cases, and its Chardonnay is especially well regarded.

Alameda County and Livermore Valley Wineries

Around the Bay in Emeryville is Edmonds St. John Winery. This winemaker buys grapes from others or brings fruit from its own Gold Country vineyards to produce both specific varietal wines such as Mourvèdre and Grenache as well as special blends from a variety of grapes.

In Sunol stands the historic Elliston Vineyards that, a century ago, stretched over 150 acres. Prohibition killed the Elliston business, and it was not until other owners revived it first in the early 1980s and again in the early 1990s that it has come back. Elliston marries its wine with fine food, serving dinners at its seventeen-room, 1890s mansion Friday and Saturday evenings by reservation only.

To the west in Alameda County is the legendary Livermore Valley. Growers have raised grapes here since the 1880s, and California's well-known John Concannon, Carl Wente, and Charles Wetmore's Cresta Blanca wineries here are among the state's oldest. The Wente family acquired the Cresta Blanca vineyards in 1981 and Concannon Vineyard in 1992. Now in their fourth and fifth generation, the Wentes have been operating a winery longer than any other family in California. Their tour takes visitors past hundred-year-old redwood barrels favored long ago because, unlike oak, the redwood imparted no flavor to the wines aging inside.

San Francisco Bay Selection
Left to right: Elliston 2000 Sunol Valley Vineyard Pinot Gris; Elliston 1997 Captain's Claret; Bonny Doon 1997 Original Zinfandel; Bonny Doon 1999 Ca del Solo Big House Red; Wente 1999 Rivera Ranch Reserve Arroyo Seco Monterey Chardonnay; Wente 1997 Livermore Cabernet Sauvignon; J. Lohr 1999 Riverstone Monterey Chardonnay; J. Lohr 1999 Seven Oaks, Paso Robles Cabernet Sauvignon

Contra Costa County Vineyards

Northeast of Alameda County is Contra Costa, a region that was home, until 1919 and the start of Prohibition, to twenty-seven wineries with 6,000 acres of grapes dating back to 1846. Christian Brothers started here and the Italian Swiss Colony grew great grapes in the area. Today, the land is so valuable for residential and commercial use that few vineyards remain. Sonoma's Cline Cellars operates one of the county's best known remaining vineyards, Bridgehead in Oakley.

Santa Clara County Wineries

To the south is Santa Clara County, which includes the greater San Jose area and home to some of California's well-regarded winemakers and some of the state's most historic. Paul Masson and his father-in-law, Charles Lefranc, became partners in 1892, planted the celebrated La Cresta vineyard, and produced wines together until Masson sold out in 1936 to Martin Ray, who in turn sold to Seagram in 1942. Under Seagram, Masson wines expanded greatly. Today, Masson's celebrity is replaced by the new work done by vigorous winemakers, most of whom buy grapes from surrounding counties.

Murrieta's Well
The winery building is more than a century old and was named for an artesian well just in front of it. The property was the frequent hiding place of legendary Gold Rush–era outlaw Joaquin Murrieta. Acquiring the property in 1884, Frenchman Louis Mel named his new winery after the local legend.

Be sure to visit David Bruce Winery, Byington Winery, and Testarossa Vineyards in Los Gatos; Cinnabar Vineyards & Winery, Clos LaChance Winery, Cooper-Garrod Estate Vineyards, and Kathryn Kennedy (who makes Cabernet Sauvignon only and tastes by appointment only) in Saratoga; Cronin Vineyards and Woodside Vineyards in Woodside; Fellom Ranch Vineyards, Picchetti Winery (formerly Sunrise Winery), and Ridge Vineyards in Cupertino; and don't miss Thomas Fogarty Winery in Portola Valley.

Santa Cruz County

A few miles south of San Jose, one enters Santa Cruz County, home to several other fine winemakers, starting with Randall Grahm at Bonny Doon Vineyard. Grahm, who calls himself a perpetual liberal arts student, is still a perpetual student of wines and winemaking. He is known as one of the industry's most vibrant creators.

Also visit Fortino Winery for old-style Italian wines in Gilroy; Storr's Winery and Santa Cruz Mountain Vineyard in Santa Cruz; Sycamore Creek Vineyards and Emilio Guglielmo Winery in Morgan Hill; and Salamandre Wine Cellars in Aptos.

Unlike wineries in Napa and Sonoma, many of these are small, family-run operations, and you'll need an appointment to visit and taste. Do make the effort, though, as many of these winemakers produce some of the state's finest wines.

Wente Vineyards

German immigrant Carl Wente purchased forty-eight acres of land in the Livermore Valley east of San Francisco Bay and established a winery in 1883. Early California winemakers favored redwood barrels rather than oak because redwood imparted no flavor to the aging wines inside them, desirable for the kinds of wines Wente first produced. The winery at Wente Vineyards is a mix of history and state-of-the-art technology. Wente made sacramental wines during Prohibition and resumed commercial production afterward. In 2000, the fifth generation joined the firm, making Wente the longest continuously running winery in the United States.

Elliston Vineyards

While original owner Henry Ellis planted grapes in the 1890s and built the seventeen-room three-story house afterward, Keith and Donna Flavetta, current owners of Elliston Vineyards, re-established the winery as a way to finance the restoration of the mansion. Most of Elliston's 5,700-case output goes to the mansion for sale through the tasting room, or it is served on Friday and Saturday evenings to the ninety or so diners who come for the single-seating five-course fixed-price meals.

San Francisco Bay Area Winery and Vineyard Resources

Marin County

Kalin Cellars
61 Galli Drive
Novato, CA 94949
415-883-3543
www.kalincellars.com
By appointment only

Alameda County

Cedar Mountain Winery
7000 Tesla Road
Livermore, CA 94550
925-373-6636
www.wines.com/cedarmountain
Sat–Sun 12–4

Concannon Vineyard
4890 Tesla Road
Livermore, CA 94550
925-456-2505
www.concannonvineyard.com
Daily 11:00–4:30

Edmonds St. John Winery
1331 Walnut Street
Berkeley, CA 94709
510-981-1510
www.edmundsstjohn.com
By appointment only

Elliston Vineyards
463 Kilkare Road
Sunol, CA 94586
925-862-2377
www.elliston.com
Fri–Sun 11–5 June–August
Sat–Sun 11–5 September–May

Fenestra Winery
83 Vallecitos Road
Livermore, CA 94550
925-862-2292
www.fenestrawinery.com
Sat–Sun 12–5

Livermore Valley Cellars
1508 Wetmore Road
Livermore, CA 94550
925-447-1751
Daily 12–5

Murrieta's Well
3005 Mines Road
Livermore, CA 94550
925-456-2390
www.murrietaswell.com
Fri–Sun 11:00–4:30

Retzlaff Vineyards
1356 S. Livermore Avenue
Livermore, CA 94550
925-447-8941
www.retzlaffwinery.com
Tues–Fri 12–2
Sat–Sun 12:00–4:30

Rosenblum Cellars
2900 Main Street
Alameda, CA 94501
510-865-7007
www.rosenblumcellars.com
Daily 12–5

Stony Ridge Winery
4948 Tesla Road
Livermore, CA 94550
925-449-0458
www.stonyridgewinery.com
Daily 11:00–4:30

Tamas Estates and Steven Kent
     Winery
5443 Tesla Road
Livermore, CA 94550
925-456-2380
www.ivantamas.com
Daily 12:00–4:30

Thomas Coyne Winery
51 East Valecitos Road
Livermore, CA 94550
925-373-6541
Sat–Sun 12–5

Wente Vineyards
5565 Tesla Road
Livermore, CA 94550
925-456-2300
www.wentevineyards.com
Daily 11:00–4:30

Santa Clara County

Byington Winery
21850 Bear Creek Road
Los Gatos, CA 95033
408-354-1111
www.byington.com
Daily 11–5

David Bruce Winery
21439 Bear Creek Road
Los Gatos, CA 95030
www.davidbrucewinery.com
408-354-4214
Mon–Fri 11–5
Sat–Sun 11:00–5:30

Cinnabar Vineyards & Winery
23000 Congress Springs Road
Saratoga, CA 95071
408-741-5858
www.cinnabarwine.com
Not open to public

Clos LaChance Winery
1 Hummingbird Lane
San Martin, CA 95046
800-487-9463
www.clos.com
Daily 10–4

Cooper-Garrod Estate Vineyards
22600 Mt. Eden Road
Saratoga, CA 95070
408-741-8094
www.cgv.com
Wed–Fri 1–5
Sat–Sun 11–5

Cronin Vineyards
11 Old La Honda Road
Woodside, CA 94062
650-851-1452
By appointment only

Fellom Ranch Vineyards
17075 Monte Bello Road
Cupertino, CA 95014
408-741-0307
By appointment only

J. Lohr Winery
1000 Lenzen Avenue
San Jose, CA 95126
408-288-5057
www.jlohr.com
Daily 10–5

Kathryn Kennedy Winery
13180 Pierce Road
Saratoga, CA 95070
408-867-4170
By appointment only

Mirassou Vineyards
3000 Aborn Road
San Jose, CA 95135
408-274-4000
www.mirassou.com
Daily 12–5

Picchetti Winery
(formerly Sunrise Winery)
13100 Monte Bello Road
Cupertino, CA 95014
408-741-1310
www.picchetti.com
Daily 11–5

Ridge Vineyards
17100 Monte Bello Road
Cupertino, CA 95015
408-867-3233
www.ridgewine.com
Sat–Sun 11–4

Savannah Chanelle Vineyards
(formerly Mariani Vineyards)
23600 Congress Springs
Saratoga, CA 95070
408-741-2934
www.savannahchanelle.com
Daily 11–5

Testarossa Vineyards
Bien Nacido Vineyard
300-A College Avenue
Los Gatos, CA 95030
408-354-6150
www.testarossa.com
By appointment only

Thomas Fogarty Winery
Skyline Boulevard
Portola Valley, CA 94028
650-851-6777
www.fogartywinery.com
Thu–Sun 11–5

Woodside Vineyards
340 Kings Mountain Road
Woodside, CA 94062
650-851-3144
www.woodsidevineyards.com
By appointment only

Santa Cruz County

Bonny Doon Vineyards
10 Pine Flat Road
Santa Cruz, CA 95060
831-425-3625
www.bonnydoonvineyards.com
Daily 11–5 except major holidays

Fortino Winery
4525 Hecker Pass Highway
Gilroy, CA 95020
408-842-3305
www.fortinowinery.com
Mon–Sat 10–5
Sun 12–5

Guglielmo Winery
1480 East Main Avenue
Morgan Hill, CA 95037
408-779-2145
www.guglielmowinery.com
Daily 10–5

Salamandre Wine Cellars
108 Don Carlos Drive
Aptos, CA 95003
831-685-0321
By appointment only

Santa Cruz Mountain Vineyard
2300 Jarvis Road
Santa Cruz, CA 95065
831-426-6209
www.scmvwines.com
By appointment only

Storr's Winery
3303 Potrero Street
Santa Cruz, CA 95060
831-458-5030
Thu–Mon 12–5

Sycamore Creek Vineyards
12775 Uvas Road
Morgan Hill, CA 95037
408-779-4738
Sat–Sun 11:30–5:00 by appointment

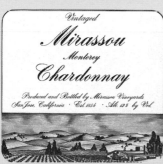

San Francisco Bay Area's Best Wine and Wineries

Bonny Doon Pinot Meunier
Bonny Doon Syrahs
Cinnabar Chardonnays
Cline Cellars Zinfandels
Cronin Vineyards Cabernet Sauvignons
David Bruce Zinfandels
Ivan Tamas Cabernet Sauvignons
J. Lohr Reserve Cabernet Sauvignons
Kalin Cellars Chardonnays
Kalin Cellars Reserve Sauvignon Blanc
Kalin Cellars Semillons
Ridge Santa Cruz Chardonnays
Ridge Zinfandels
Rosenblum Cellars Zinfandels

Chapter Eight

The Vast Central Valley

The Viticultural Heartland of California

Looking at a map, this huge central expanse of California stretches from Bakersfield in the south, past Sacramento, and on up north of Shasta Lake, nearly 400 miles along Interstate 5 and California Highway 99. This area consists of three major growing areas: Lodi, Modesto, and Fresno, as well as some smaller districts. Although this vast area houses many fewer wineries than Napa or Sonoma, more than 70 percent of the state's wine output comes from those who call this area home. Yet while the Central Valley is a vast region of large vineyards, few of its wineries are open to the public for tasting or tours.

As with every other region, its climate provides expectations and yields a few contradictions. Through the San Joaquin Valley beginning far south of Lodi up to the Sacramento Valley north of the state's capital city, the area is known for scorching hot summer days with high temperatures above 100 degrees from late July through September. Though the winters can be downright cold, with temperatures dipping into the teens overnight, with few exceptions, it is the summer heat and sunlight that defines the region's winemaking capabilities and how grape growers deal with it. The exceptions—such as Clarksburg's Bogle Winery, just south of Sacramento in the Sacramento River Delta, and those growers around Lodi—benefit from the temperature modulating effects of San Francisco Bay's long arms.

East-northeast of Sacramento in Esparto, R. H. Phillips produces well-liked Rhône varietals and its Toasted Head Chardonnay is popular. Just south of Sacramento off California Highway 84, Bogle is nestled along the Sacramento River in a micro-climate strongly influenced by the cooling effect of the delta. The Bogle family is now in its sixth generation farming in central California, and raises nearly 1,200 acres of grapes on nearby Merritt Island. Bogle's moderately priced Petite Sirah has been its flagship varietal since 1979, and its old-growth Zinfandel and Merlot are well regarded.

Travelers on Highway 99 will notice that vines are trellised differently along California's Agriculture Belt from the way growers trellis vines in Napa, Sonoma, or Mendocino. To protect grapes from sunburn, growers here string the leafy vines along high wires. This allows the leaves to grow out, providing shade for the grapes. The heat that still penetrates the leaf cover encourages full ripeness and high sweetness. But the heat also cooks out acids that other regions retain to provide for more balanced and complexly flavored wines. Most of this Central Valley is categorized as Region V in the system that analyzes growing regions by heat-degree days.

Lodi Area Vineyards and Wineries

The region around Lodi is a remarkable viticultural region. It is cooled by San Francisco Bay air blown up the Carquinez Strait, the long tendril of the Bay that stretches north around Berkeley and squeezes past Vallejo and pushes another forty miles east. At its farthest extreme, the Lodi area is subject to the sponge-like river delta formed by the San Joaquin River on the south and Sacramento River on the north, affecting Clarksburg among others. The cooling effect is remarkably effective since it is barely ten miles away. This gives Lodi grape growers opportunities that those farther north or south can't enjoy.

Previous page:
E. & J. Gallo Winery
Lights burn into the evening in Ernest and Julio Gallo's Research Center building at their Modesto headquarters. Gallo, the world's largest wine producer, works tirelessly to improve flavor and quality. Under special lamps they experiment with lengthening the growing day and controlling grape-growth factors.

Central Valley Selection
Left to right: R. H. Phillips Toasted Head 1999 Dunningan Hills Chardonnay; Turning Leaf (Gallo) 1998 North Coast Coastal Reserve Pinot Noir; E. & J. Gallo Twin Valley Sauvignon Blanc; Woodbridge (Mondavi) 1999 California Chardonnay; Ficklin Madera port; Monterra (Delicato) 1998 Monterey Merlot; Delicato 1998 San Bernabe Vine Select Syrah; Bogle 1999 California Old Vine Zinfandel; Bogle 1999 California Petite Syrah

More than 600 growers raise more than 75,000 acres of grapes around Lodi, selling Cabernet Sauvignon, Merlot, Chardonnay, Sauvignon Blanc, and Zinfandel grapes to winemakers locally and statewide.

About fifteen miles south of Lodi in Manteca is Delicato Vineyards. Grape growing dates back to 1924 when founder Gaspare Indelicato arrived in California. Through the next decade, he expanded his vineyard in Manteca to 124 acres. A year after Prohibition's repeal, Gaspare, who had Americanized his nickname as Jasper, collaborated with his brother-in-law Sebastiano "Sam" Luppino to found Sam-Jasper Winery. While they struggled through the Great Depression, they held on, and over time they began making wines for other growers and even other winemakers.

In 1974, the Indelicato family changed the company name to Delicato, and soon after acquired and planted a 1,600-acre parcel of land near Lodi, their Clay Station Vineyard. Success with Delicato's own White Zinfandel allowed it to expand, and in 1988, the winery acquired San Bernabe Vineyards in Monterey County from Prudential Insurance, giving Delicato grapes grown in several regions to create wines. Delicato's comfortable visitor center along Highway 99 offers tours and tastings as well as materials to aid and educate the home producer.

Bogle Winery
The Bogle family, now in its sixth generation farming in central California, grows nearly 1,200 acres on their farm south of Sacramento on Merritt Island in the river delta. Their micro-climate is cooled by the converging rivers. Just below their tasting rooms, Chardonnay grapes ripen before harvest.

Modesto Area Wineries

The remarkable Gallo family are central figures in the history of California wine. The gamble that young Ernest and Julio Gallo played during Prohibition to keep their juice until they could sell it as wine again began in a small rented warehouse in Modesto. Today, the Gallos' Modesto facility has made them the largest wine producers in the world, with output of more than 80 million cases a year.

The Gallos' philosophy has been to "make wines with flavors that appeal to many people, and do it reliably." This mission has served them well. They innovated both flavored, sweetened beverages and winemaking techniques that broke new ground. Determining that wooden barrels could never be kept scrupulously clean, they began using in the 1960s only stainless steel or glass-lined steel tanks. Gallo now has several tanks with capacities of more than 1 million gallons.

Vast quantities are normal with Gallo. While the family owns a nearly 6,000-acre vineyard west of Livingston between Modesto and Merced, those vines produce nowhere near enough grapes for all the Gallo products, and they buy thousands of tons of grapes from growers as far away as Mendocino. The recent acclaim of the Gallo of Sonoma wines speaks clearly of the adaptability and wisdom of the family. The Gallos are, however, publicity shy, and tours of the facility are rare and available only by invitation.

San Bernabe Vineyards

San Bernabe uses hundreds of hand pickers to custom-harvest grapes for its many clients. Here, a harvester gathers Pinot Blanc for Templeton's Wild Horse Winery just after a light rainstorm moved over the vineyard. Light rains are no problem but a heavy rain can affect flavor and even damage grapes.

Central Valley Winery and Vineyard Resources

Bogle Winery
37783 County Road 144
Clarksburg, CA 95612
916-744-1139
www.boglewinery.com
Mon–Fri 10–5
Sat–Sun 11–5

Delicato Vineyards and San
  Bernabe Vineyards
12001 South Highway 99
Manteca, CA 95336
209-824-3600
www.delicato.com
Daily 9:00–5:30

E. & J. Gallo Winery
600 Yosemite Blvd
Modesto, CA 95354
209-341-3054
www.gallo.com
Not open to the public

Ficklin Vineyards
30246 Avenue 7½
Madera, CA 93637
559-674-4598
www.ficklin.com
Mon–Fri 8–5
Tours by appointment

Lucas Winery
18196 N. Davis Road
Lodi, CA 95240
209-368-2006
www.lucaswinery.com
Thu–Sun 12–5

Mondavi Woodbridge
5950 East Woodbridge Road
Acampo, CA 95220
209-369-5861
www.robertmondavi.com
Tues–Sun 10:30–4:30
Tours by appointment, call 209-
  365 2839

Oak Ridge Vineyards
Eastside Winery
6100 East Highway 12
Lodi, CA 95240
209-369-4768
www.oakridgevineyards.com
Daily 12–5

Peirano Estate Vineyards
21831 North Acampo Road
Acampo, CA 95220
209-369-9463
www.peirano.com
Fri–Sun 10–5

R. H. Phillips
26836 County Road 12A
Esparto, CA 95627
530-662-3215
www.rhphillips.com
Daily 11–5

Quady Winery
13181 Road 24
Madera, CA 93637
559-673-8068
www.quadywinery.com
Mon–Fri 8:30–4:30
Sat 12:00–4:30

Winters Winery
15 Main Street
Winters, CA 95694
530-795-3201
Tasting by appointment

Wooden Valley Winery
4756 Suisun Valley Road
Suisun City, CA 94585
707-864-0730
www.woodenvalley.com
Tues–Sun 9–5

Delicato Vineyards
A harvesting machine works through a Delicato vineyard near Sacramento at daybreak.

Chapter Nine

Gold Country

The Foothills Counties Wineries

Ambitious immigrant gold prospectors charged into what would become Amador, El Dorado, and Calaveras Counties east of Sacramento during the heady days of the California Gold Rush. For only a few years and for only a few thousand individuals, gold mining proved successful. For the rest, they had little choice but to return to what they knew, to the work they did before they packed up and headed west. Many were tradespeople, but most were farmers and their ethnic backgrounds included raising grapes and producing wine.

Grape growing started early in these parts. By 1860, there were more acres planted in Amador County than in Napa. Within twenty years, there were more than 10,000 acres planted and 160 wineries in Amador and El Dorado Counties.

While grape growers in this region are successfully raising Cabernet Sauvignon, Cabernet Franc, Merlot, Syrah, Barbera, and Sangiovese grapes, the area is best known for its Zinfandels. In fact, Napa Valley's Bob Trinchero at Sutter Home was among the first to recognize just how fine the Amador Zinfandel wines were. In the late 1960s, Trinchero made wines from Amador grapes with great success, leading to the creation and enormous success of Sutter Home's white Zinfandel.

Growers raise grapes from as low as 1,000 to as high as 3,400 feet of elevation. The roads from winery to vineyard to town wander along old cow paths and streambeds, following the contours in a sometimes twisty, convoluted fashion. The drive, the scenery, and the wines are worth it all. Because of the elevations, temperatures generally are ten to twenty degrees cooler than the nearby valleys. Yet the grapes up here get the sun of the valleys without the heat while also getting the coolness of the coast without its dark fog.

Yuba County Wineries

At the far north end, in an area known as North Yuba, is the steeply sloped and terraced 365-acre Renaissance Vineyard & Winery, founded in 1971 by a philosophical group known as the Fellowship of Friends in a small town called Oregon House. Dr. Karl Werner, the founding winemaker for Callaway Winery in Temecula, came for a retreat and stayed on to guide the group's first steps.

Oregon House is quite a jaunt from the rest of the Gold Country wineries and about eighty-five miles from Sacramento, but this group has made a serious financial investment and put in twenty years of labor organically farming their 135,000 vines. Their vineyards are spread among eighty-five micro-climates, and nearly half of the grapes are Cabernet Sauvignon. They are intent on producing good wine. And as if that were not enough, Renaissance contains a fine museum of European art and furnishings dating to the seventeenth century.

Gold Country Selection
Left to right: Smith 1997 Sierra Foothill Cabernet Sauvignon; Smith 1997 Sierra Foothills Merlot; Shenandoah Vineyard 1999 Amador County Zinfandel; Sobon Estate 1999 Rocky Top Zinfandel; Sobon Estate 1999 Fiddletown Lot 1 Zinfandel; Shenandoah Vineyard 1998 Daphne Late Harvest Sauvignon Blanc; Sierra Vista 1999 El Dorado Viognier; Sierra Vista 1997 El Dorado 5 Star Reserve Syrah.

Nevada County Wineries

In Nevada County, almost due east of Oregon House in Nevada City, there is Nevada City Winery in the old foundry/garage behind the city's Art Deco fire station, and, just south in Grass Valley, the much smaller Smith Vineyard & Winery, farming organically and making wine in its small red barn. These are the two northernmost wineries in the foothills of the Sierra Nevada mountains.

El Dorado County Wineries

Separated from North Yuba and Nevada by Placer County and the main route to Lake Tahoe from San Francisco, is El Dorado County, the heart of Gold Rush territory. The American River nearly bisects the county.

The oldest winery in El Dorado County was started in 1872 by Giovanni Lombardo, who came to the area from Switzerland during the Gold Rush. Following Prohibition, it was the Boeger family that first found the soils productive, planting vines in 1972. The Boeger winery is in Placerville, along with its tasting room, which is the former Lombardo winery.

Also in Placerville are Gold Hill Vineyard, Lava Cap Winery, and just outside of town, Sierra Vista Winery & Vineyards with its view of the Sierra's Crystal Range.

Sierra Vista's John MacCready, an electrical engineer from Ohio, and his wife, Barbara, with a masters degree in statistics, planted their first five acres of Cabernet vines in 1974, intending to sell what they grew. Ironically, their first bottling, in 1977, came from grapes they purchased as they sorted out what would grow on the 2,800-foot-elevation hillsides.

Now, John MacCready raises Zinfandel, Sauvignon Blanc, Viognier, and several Rhône varieties. He is one of an enthusiastic group of Rhône winemakers who call themselves the Rhône Rangers. The vineyard and winery satisfies his inclination toward creativity, yet it still is definitely a scientific enterprise. Now daughter Michelle, with a bachelor degree in biology and graduate classes at U.C.

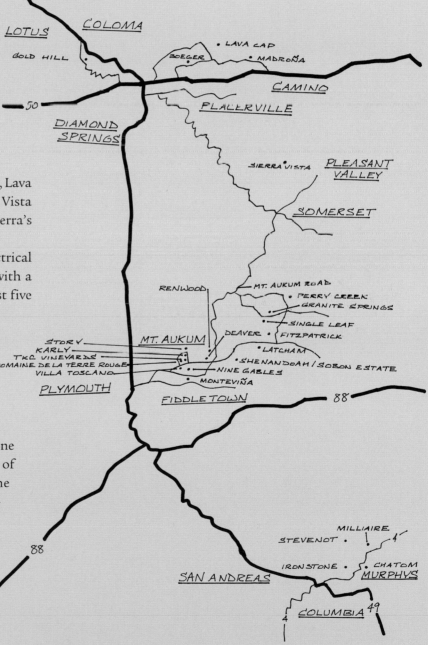

Amador, El Dorado and Calaveras Wine Country

Davis, has joined the family business that produces about 10,000 cases a year.

Just east of Placerville in Camino is Madroña Vineyard, home of legendary Zinfandels and such flavorful German grapes as Gewürztraminer. South and east of Placerville is Fair Play, home to Fitzpatrick Winery, Granite Springs Winery, Perry Creek Vineyards, and Single Leaf Vineyards. At the southern end of the county in Mt. Aukum is Latcham Vineyards.

Amador County Wineries

In the mid 1800s, Amador County led Napa in vineyards, but following Prohibition, only the D'Agostini Winery remained in the county. Founded in 1856, D'Agostini is now owned and operated by Leon Sobon.

Sobon is a brilliant experimenter. A former experimental engineer in materials sciences at the aviation leader Lockheed, he continues to devise and develop new grape varieties and new techniques for winemaking. "When you try new grapes," Sobon says, "you can't just automatically use old techniques." Do visit Sobon's Shenandoah Vineyards & Sobon Estate and the understated but fascinating museum and comfortable tasting room. Not only are the wines excellent but the selection of books covers not only wine and food but also early California history.

In Ione, there is Clos du Lac, and in Sutter Creek, there is Stoneridge.

In and around Plymouth, up and down the Shenandoah Valley, there is Amador Foothill Winery, Deaver Vineyards, Domaine de la Terre Rouge, Karly Wines, Monteviña Winery, Nine Gables Vineyards, Renwood Winery, Story Winery, TKC Vineyards, Villa Toscano Winery, and Vino Noceto.

Calaveras County Wineries

Continuing south and crossing into Calaveras County, Murphys is home to several wineries including Black Sheep Vintners, Milliaire Winery, Stevenot Winery (Calaveras County's first to open after Prohibition, in 1978), and, of course, John Kautz's Ironstone Vineyards.

Kautz is California's eighth-largest grape grower, raising 4,200 acres, only 70 of them in the foothills regions, the rest in the Central Valley. Ironstone is a destination in itself, with its mining museum, bakery, delicatessen, and a park with a waterfall. The winery itself is quite a showplace.

Tuolumne County Wineries

Last but not least is Sonora Winery & Port Works in Sonora, in Tuolumne County. This small establishment specializes in Zinfandels and Ports made from various Portuguese varietals.

Travel directions
All around Plymouth in Amador County, you can still find wineries by following signs like this even if you have neither map nor cell phone nor GPS. Amador, and Calaveras County to the south, as well as El Dorado and Placer Counties to the north, are some of California's more productive grape-growing and winemaking regions.

Nevada City Winery
Just off Broad Street in Nevada City, the Nevada City Winery has taken over an old foundry and auto repair shop. It is located on Spring Street just opposite the Art Deco fire station and behind the city hall. Its small tasting room is comfortable and stylish.

Gold Country's Best Wines and Wineries

Amador Foothill Zinfandels
Boeger Zinfandels
Karly Cellars Sauvignon Blancs
Monteviña Cabernet Sauvignons
Nevada City Cabernet Sauvignons
Renwood Zinfandels
Shenandoah Sobon Estate Zinfandels
Shenandoah Vineyards Cabernet
    Sauvignons
Sierra Vista Cabernet Sauvignons
Sierra Vista Zinfandels
Stevenot Cabernet Sauvignons

Left images:

Ironstone Vineyards

Ironstone has become a tourist destination as much as a winery, offering entertainment, food, an interesting museum of mining, and a gift shop that celebrates the foothills regions and their historical contribution to California history. From a museum of mining to a classic car show to an outdoor amphitheater drawing major entertainers, John Kautz has done as much as any other winery owner to promote his facility and his products. Kautz is also California's eighth-largest grape grower, with about 4,100 acres in vines near Lodi in California's Central Valley and about 70 acres around his winery in Murphys.

Left:

Smith Vineyard & Winery

Smith Vineyard & Winery raises organically grown Chardonnay in its hilltop fields. New owners Joseph and Melissa Damiano also produce a Chenin Blanc and Cabernet Sauvignon from their organic vineyards. Organic vineyards require more personal attention, and most organic winemakers walk all of their rows every week, catching conditions before they become problems. The Damianos produce about 2,000 cases each year from the red barn at the rear of their property.

Shenandoah Vineyards

The oldest existing winery in the Sierra foothills was started by Adam Uhlinger in 1856 in Shenandoah Valley, near Plymouth. Within two decades, Uhlinger sold out to the D'Agostini family. Eventually, retired Lockheed engineer Leon Sobon acquired the winery, turning the old stone structure into a fine museum. Sobon has made a strong reputation producing Zinfandels from his Fiddletown 1910s-era vineyard and from his Rocky Top and Cougar Hill vineyards first planted in the 1920s. He started out driving his wine-filled station wagon from restaurant to restaurant selling his cases.

Gold Rush Country Winery and Vineyard Resources

Amador County

Amador Foothill Winery
12500 Steiner Road
Plymouth, CA 95669
209-245-6307
www.amadorfoothill.com
Fri–Sun 12–5 and most holidays

Clos du Lac Cellars
Greenstone Winery
3153 Highway 88
Ione, CA 95640
209-274-2238
www.closdulac.com
Wed–Sun 10–5

Deaver Vineyards
12455 Steiner Road
Plymouth, CA 95669
209-245-4099
www.deavervineyards.com
Daily 11–5

Domaine de la Terre Rouge
Easton Wines
10801 Dickson Road
Plymouth, CA 95669
209-245-4277
www.terrerougewines.com
Fri–Sun 11–4

Karly Wines
11076 Bell Road
Plymouth, CA 95669
209-245-3922
www.karlywines.com
Daily 12–4

Monteviña Winery
20680 Shenandoah School Road
Plymouth, CA 95669
209-245-6942
www.montevina.com
Daily 10:00–4:30 except major
holidays

Nine Gables Vineyard
10778 Shenandoah Road
Plymouth, CA 95669
www.ninegables.com
209-245-3949
Thur–Sun 11–5 or by appointment

Renwood Winery
12225 Steiner Road
Plymouth, CA 95669
209-245-6979
www.renwood.com
Daily 10:30–5:30

Shenandoah Vineyards & Sobon
Estate
12300 Steiner Road
Plymouth, CA 95669
209-245-4455
www.sobonwine.com
Daily 10–5

Story Winery
10525 Bell Road
Plymouth, CA 95669
209-245-6208
www.zin.com
Mon–Fri 12–4
Sat–Sun 11–5

TKC Vineyards
11001 Valley Drive
Plymouth, CA 95669
209-245-6428
www.amadorwine.com
Sat 11–5
Sun 1–5 or by appointment

Villa Toscano Winery
10600 Shenandoah Road
Plymouth, CA 95669
209-245-3800
www.villatoscano.com
Daily 10–5

Vino Noceto
11011 Shenandoah Road
Plymouth, CA 95669
209-245-6556
www.noceto.com
Fri–Sun 11–4 and by appointment

Calaveras County

Chatom Vineyards
1969 Highway 4
Douglas Flat, CA 95229
209-736-6500
www.chatomvineyards.com
Daily 11–5

Kautz Ironstone Vineyards
1894 Six Mile Road
Murphys, CA 95247
209-728-1251
www.ironstonevineyards.com
Daily 10–6

Milliaire Winery
276 Main Street
Murphys, CA 95247
209-728-1658
www.milliairewinery.com
Daily 11–5

Stevenot Winery
458 Main Street
Murphys, CA 95247
831-728-0148
or at winery at:
2690 San Domingo Road
Murphys, CA 95247
209-728-0638
www.stevenotwinery.com
Daily 10–5

El Dorado County

Boeger Winery
1709 Carson Road
Placerville, CA 95667
530-622-8094
www.boegerwinery.com
Daily 10–5

Fitzpatrick Winery & Lodge
7740 Fair Play Road
Fair Play, CA 95684
800-245-9166
www.fitzpatrickwinery.com
Fri–Mon 11–5

Gold Hill Vineyard
5660 Vineyard Lane
Placerville, CA 95667
530-626-6522
www.goldhillvineyard.com
Thur–Sun 10–5

Granite Springs Winery &
Vineyards
5050 Granite Springs Winery
Road
Fair Play, CA 95684
530-620-6395
Daily 11–5

Latcham Vineyards
2860 Omo Ranch Road
Mount Aukum, CA 95656
530-620-6834
Daily 11–5

Lava Cap Winery
2221 Fruitridge Road
Placerville, CA 95667
530-621-0175
www.lavacap.com
Daily 11–5

Madroña Vineyards
High Hill Road
Camino, CA 95709
530-644-5948
www.madrona-wines.com
Daily 11–5

Perry Creek Vineyards
7400 Perry Creek Road
Fair Play, CA 95684
530-620-5175
www.perrycreek.com
Wed–Sun 11–5

Sierra Vista Winery & Vineyards
4560 Cabernet Way
Placerville, CA 95667
530-622-7221
www.sierravistawinery.com
Daily 10–5

Single Leaf Vineyards
7480 Fair Play Road
Fair Play, CA 95684
530-620-3545
www.singleleaf.com
Fri–Sun 11–5

Nevada County

Nevada City Winery
321 Spring Street
Nevada City, CA 95959
530-265-9463
Mon–Sat 11–5
Sun 12–5

Smith Vineyard & Winery
13719 Dog Bar Road
Grass Valley, CA 95949
530-273-7032
By appointment only

Tuolumne County

Sonora Winery & Port Works
17500 Route 5 Road
Sonora, CA 95370
209-532-7678
www.sonorawinery.com
Sat–Sun 11:00–4:30
Weekdays by appointment

Yuba County

Renaissance Vineyards & Winery
12585 Rice's Crossing Road
Oregon House, CA 95962
530-692-2222
www.rvw.com
Fri–Sat by appointment

Chapter Ten

Monterey County

Wineries in Paradise

Grape growing in Monterey dates back to the Franciscan fathers of the Mission Soledad, who planted Mission grapes in the 1800s. But when the Spanish government secularized the missions, grape growing disappeared from Monterey County for nearly 150 years. It wasn't until 1961, when Edmund Mirassou first planted 300 acres, that grape growers began to recognize the favorable climate conditions the county offered.

In quick succession, Paul Masson, owned then by Seagram, planted 1,000 acres near Greenfield in 1962, and Mirassou added another 900. A year later, Carl Wente planted 700 acres in Arroyo Seco. The frenzy began, aided by tax-shelter incentives. Masson added 4,500 acres more around Greenfield, Almaden planted 2,000 acres, and Prudential planted San Bernabe, the world's largest single vineyard at 7,500 acres, just south of King City. Under Delicato's current ownership, San Bernabe has expanded to its full potential with 8,500 acres of varietals.

Monterey's climate favors white grapes. The area's warm sun raises temperatures, and the resulting low pressure draws in heavier, cooler ocean air and fog. Later in the summer, strong winds blow the length of the valley, cooling the potentially overheated grapes. Yet this eighty-mile-long valley gets much warmer the farther south one travels. White grapes flourish also in the valley near Salinas and farther north; this area is home to 40 percent of the Riesling and 50 percent of the Sauvignon Blanc grapes in the entire state.

Red grapes grow well in the bottom third of the valley around San Lucas and farther south. Growers raise other Cabernets in the Carmel Valley and in the Santa Lucia highlands.

Visiting Monterey County wineries is certainly no hardship and makes for a wonderful vacation destination, as delightful as any journey through Napa and Sonoma. Many of the county's finest wineries are in Carmel Valley and the surrounding area, where the dinnertime dilemma is what wonderful restaurant to sample there or in nearby Monterey, Pacific Grove, or Carmel.

Carmel Valley Wineries

Among the top wineries is Bernardus Winery in Carmel Valley. Owner Ben Pon was a talented and successful international race-car driver as well as a Dutch wine merchant when he established Bernardus (his given name) in 1989. Farther east in the Carmel Valley, he has planted Cabernet, Merlot, Cab Franc, Petit Verdot, and Sauvignon Blanc, and he buys Chardonnay and Sauvignon Blanc grapes from warmer climes. His wines are well regarded. Pon has recently opened a luxurious lodge in the valley as well.

Also in the Carmel Valley, visit Chateau Julien, Durney Vineyards, Georis Winery, Joullian Vineyards, and Talbott Vineyards, all in close proximity to one another.

While in the Carmel Valley, do not miss Galante Vineyards. This beautiful ranch is also the home of Galante Garden Roses and some 12,000 bushes in ninety varieties bloom there, surrounded by hundreds of live oak trees shading the 700-acre property. The thirty-minute drive, east on Carmel Valley Road and up and over two passes on Cachagua Road,

Monterey County Selection
Left to right: Georis 1997 Carmel Valley Merlot; Bernardus 1996 Bien Nacido Santa Barbara County Pinot Noir; Galante 1998 Carmel Valley Red Rose Cabernet Sauvignon; Galante 1999 Carmel Valley Black Jack Pasture Cabernet Sauvignon; Galante 2000 Carmel Valley Sauvignon Blanc; Bernardus 1997 Carmel Valley Marinus

may seem long but the effort is worthwhile and the scenery lovely. The winery, a new barn built to look old, is tidily laid out with modern equipment and oak barrels. The views from the winery and tasting room are among the finest anywhere in California's wine country.

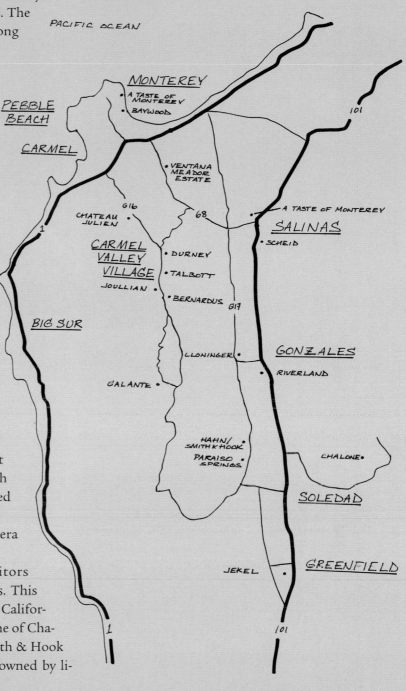

Monterey Area Wineries

In nearby Monterey, taste the wines of Baywood Cellars (formerly Las Vinas Winery) at its site on Cannery Row. Before leaving town, or in lieu of ever leaving the spectacular Monterey coast, many of the county's wines can be tasted and purchased at A Taste of Monterey on Cannery Row in Monterey or on Main Street in Salinas near the John Steinbeck Center. In fact, products from Lockwood Vineyards, Morgan Winery, Monterey Vineyards, and Pavona Wines can only be tasted at one of A Taste of Monterey's two locations.

Salinas Area Wineries and Vineyards

Heading west toward Salinas, don't miss Meador Estate and Ventana Vineyards. Then in Salinas, visit Boyer Wines and Cloninger Cellars. Not far south of Salinas in Spreckels, Rick Boyer's well-regarded wines are available by appointment.

Turning north from Salinas leads to Calera Wine Company, in Hollister.

Heading south, Highway 101 takes visitors through Gonzales, home of Riverland Vineyards. This was formerly Deere Valley Vineyards and Taylor California Cellars. Then continue south to Soledad, home of Chalone Vineyards, Paraiso Springs Winery, and Smith & Hook Winery. In Greenfield, there is Jekel Vineyards, owned by liquor giant Brown-Forman.

If you are driving south toward San Luis Obispo and Santa Barbara Counties, you might take a slight detour just before King City on Oasis Road to the impressive San Bernabe Vineyards. The winery does not offer tours and there is no tasting room, just 8,500 acres of vines. Stay on Oasis Road as it takes you through the vineyard. Watch out for vineyard vehicles, and remember that you are driving through private property so don't stop and harvest your own Sangiovese or Chenin Blanc. But as you drive through San Bernabe, remember that many wineries throughout the state—in fact, some of the best, which do have tasting rooms where you can sample their products—use grapes grown here.

Joullian Vineyards

Joullian's tasting room is known as the "castle," and its river-rock façade, gothic windows, and classic gable roofline add to the impression. The Carmel Valley Village, just a few miles inland from Monterey Bay, offers wine tasting, great food, and fine accommodations in close proximity to one another.

Georis Winery

Georis is best known for its estate Merlot, raised, fermented, aged, and bottled in its vineyards and winery twenty miles inland from the Pacific Ocean where daytime temperatures can reach 90 degrees by mid afternoon and drop to 40 at night. Georis's tasting room in the Carmel Valley Village is a whimsically cluttered garden.

Galante Vineyards

The Galante family planted its first grapes in 1983 on its ranch at an 1,800-foot elevation, and got its first harvest in 1986, selling its produce to other winemakers. Winemaker Greg Vita starts his premium Black Jack Pasture Cabernet Sauvignon in new, French-oak barrels while he ages his Rancho wines eighteen months in two- and three-year-old barrels. The winery produces just 4,000 cases a year and often as little as 25 cases of some varieties. Galante built its ranch-barn-style winery in 1994 with its first release that year.

Autumn colors
Monterey County's vineyards turn color in the fall, often aided by a late-afternoon rainstorm that may add color to the sky.
A drive along southern and central California's U.S. 101 from late September through early November can be a visual treat.

Above:

San Bernabe Vineyards

San Bernabe's vineyard manager Bill Petrovik has been on site-since 1978. He says, "Vines aren't very different from us. The older they get, the more problems show up." Like most large vineyards, San Bernabe has an ongoing program that regularly replants grape vines such these Merlot and Syrah blocks.

Right:

Monterey vista

Grape growing began in Monterey County with the arrival of Spanish missionaries at the Soledad Mission in the early 1800s. After the Spanish government secularized the missions in 1834, the friars abandoned the vines, and the land fell mainly to cattle grazing. Parts of the county look as they did in the 1830s.

Carmel Valley vista

Most visitors think of Monterey Bay and Carmel as resort areas for golf, classic car shows and races, seafood dinners on the wharf, and the stunning Monterey Aquarium. Yet the Carmel Valley is an ideal grape-growing location, warmed by daily sun and cooled by afternoon ocean breezes and fog. This west end of the valley is best known for its red-wine grapes.

Monterey County's Best Wines and Wineries

Bernardus Sauvignon Blancs
Calera Pinot Noirs
Calera Viogniers
Chalone Estate Chardonnays
Chateau Julien Cabernet Sauvignons
Chateau Julien Merlots
Durney Estate Chardonnays
Jekel Vineyards Cabernet Sauvignons
Morgan Winery Cabernet Sauvignons
Robert Talbott Estate Chardonnays
Robert Talbott Logan Chardonnays

Right:

Scheid Vineyards

In Monterey County along U.S. 101, the growth of vineyards and loss of cattle land has changed golden range into verdant rows. The enormous Scheid Vineyard, near San Lucas, shows one-, two-, and three-year-old vines surrounding the old windmill that pumped water to tanks for grazing cattle.

Monterey County Winery and Vineyard Resources

Baywood Cellars
Las Vinas Winery
381 Cannery Row Suite C
Monterey, CA 93940
831-645-9035
www.baywoodcellars.com
Daily 11-7

Bernardus Winery
5 West Carmel Valley Road
Carmel Valley, CA 93924
831-659-1900
www.bernardus.com
Daily 11-5

Boyer Wines
Salinas, CA 93962
831-455-1885
By appointment only

Calera Wine Company
11300 Cienega Road
Hollister, CA 95023
831 637 9170
By appointment only

Chalone Vineyards
Highway 146 at Stonewall
    Canyon Road
Soledad, CA 93960
831-678-1717
www.chalonevineyard.com
Sat-Sun 11-4
Weekdays by appointment

Chateau Julien
8940 Carmel Valley Road
Carmel Valley, CA 93923
831-624-2600
www.chateaujulien.com
Mon-Fri 8-5
Sat-Sun 11-5
Tours daily by appointment

Cloninger Cellars
1645 River Road
Salinas, CA 93902
831-675-9463
www.cloningerwine.com
Mon-Thur 11-4
Fri-Sun 11-5

Durney Vineyards
69 West Carmel Valley Road
Carmel Valley, CA 93924
831-659-6220
www.durneywines.com
www.hellerestate.com
Mon-Fri 11-5
Sat-Sun 10-5

Galante Vineyards
18181 Cachagua Road
Carmel Valley, CA 93924
831-659-2649
www.galantevineyards.com
Mon-Sat 11-3 by appointment
    only

Georis Winery
4 Pilot Road
Carmel Valley, CA 93024
831-659-1050
www.georiswine.com
Daily 11-5

Jekel Vineyards
40155 Walnut Avenue
Greenfield, CA 93927
831-674-5525
Daily 11-4

Joullian Vineyards
Tasting room: 2 Village Drive
    Suite A
Carmel Valley, CA 93924
831-659-8100
www.joullianvineyards.com
Daily 11-5

Lockwood Vineyard
800-753-1424
www.lockwood-wine.com
Not open to the public
Tasting at A Taste of Monterey

Meador Estate
2999 Monterey-Salinas Highway
Monterey, CA 93940
831-375-0741
www.meadorestate.com
Daily 11-5

Morgan Winery
Salinas, CA 93901
831-751-7777
www.morganwinery.com
Not open to the public
Tasting at A Taste of Monterey

Paraiso Springs Winery
38060 Paraiso Springs Road
Soledad, CA 93960
831-678-0300
www.paraisospringsvineyards.com
Mon-Fri 12-4
Sat-Sun 11-5

Pavona Wines
885 Abrego Street
Monterey, CA 93940
831-646-1506
www.pavonawines.com
Tasting at A Taste of Monterey

Riverland Vineyards
(formerly Deer Valley Vineyards
    and Taylor California Cellars)
800 South Alta Street
Gonzales, CA 93926
831-675-2481
www.cwine.com
Wed-Sun 11-4

Scheid Vineyards
305 Hilltown Road
Salinas, CA 93908
831-455-9990
www.scheidvineyards.com

Smith & Hook Winery
Hahn Estates
37700 Foothill Road
Soledad, CA 93960
831-678-2132
www.hahnestates.com
Daily 11-4

Talbott Vineyards
530 West Carmel Valley Road
Carmel Valley, CA 93924
831-659-3500
www.talbottvineyards.com
Daily 11-5 Memorial Day to
    Labor Day
Thu-Mon 11-5 Labor Day to
    Memorial Day

Ventana Vineyards
2999 Monterey-Salinas Highway
Monterey, CA 93940
831-372-7415
www.ventanawines.com
Daily 11-5

Tasting Rooms

A Taste of Monterey
700 Cannery Row
Monterey, CA 93940
831-646-5446
www.tastemonterey.com
Daily 11-6

A Taste of Monterey
127 Main Street
Salinas, CA 93901
831-751-1980
Mon-Sat 11-5

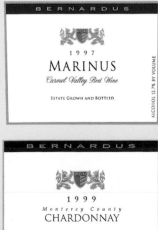

Chapter Eleven

San Luis Obispo County

Central California Wineries

This county consists of two quite different grape-growing and winemaking regions, one warm, Paso Robles, and the other surprisingly cool, the Edna Valley.

The name Paso Robles is an abbreviation of the Spanish *El Paso de Robles*, "the pass of the oaks," those magnificent trees lining Highway 101 through most of the length of California wine country. This area, basically on the east side of Highway 101, is warm, similar to Sonoma County's Alexander Valley, with similar healthy red grape crops. The Paso Robles reds have been described as soft and fleshy, with gentle tannins and a more overt fruit character. They are more charming and rich than their counterparts from northern Sonoma County.

The one climatic exception to Paso Robles's heat is around Templeton where, from the 1850s, grape growers have taken advantage of cool ocean air coming in through the Templeton Gap. Here, daytime temperatures are likely 10 degrees cooler and nights 20 degrees cooler than in Paso Robles.

Further south in the county, a few miles southeast of the city of San Luis Obispo, the Edna Valley enjoys long summer days moderated by ocean-cooled breezes and morning fog. This favors growing Chardonnay grapes, which are now nearly 70 percent of the valley's output. Still farther southeast is Arroyo Grande where both Chardonnay and Pinot Noir flourish. Similar to Mendocino County, one trend throughout San Luis Obispo County is organic farming, and a number of grape growers use no pesticides or herbicides in their vineyards.

Paso Robles Area Wineries

In Paso Robles, visit Adelaida Cellars, Arciero Estate Winery, and the recently opened EOS Estate Winery. Hope Farm Winery began in 1990, and other recent additions to this area opening in 1994 include boutique-sized Dark Star Cellars, Dunning Vineyards, and Grey Wolf Cellars.

One of Paso Robles's most entertaining tasting rooms is Tobin James, whose facility resembles an 1890s Western saloon. Tobin James's Sirah and reserve Zinfandel are well regarded.

Justin Baldwin produces well-liked wines at his Justin Vineyards & Winery, where he and his wife also operate a luxurious bed-and-breakfast. The old-Italian-sounding Fratelli Perata Winery produces modern California-style varietals. Don't miss Meridian Vineyards, owned by Beringer of Napa, which may be San Luis Obispo County's largest producer.

Other boutique producers in the area include Vista del Rey Vineyards, Windward Vineyard, Poalillo Wines, and Tablas Creek Vineyard. Each of these produces smaller quantities, some fewer than 2,000 cases, and it is well worth the effort to see and taste their wines. Their tasting hours usually are limited to weekends but they open by appointment at other times.

Larger Paso Robles wineries include Eberle Winery, Laura's Vineyard, J. Lohr Winery, Martin & Weyrich Winery, Midnight Cellars, Norman Vineyards, Sylvester Winery, and the well-regarded Peachy Canyon Winery, whose tasting room is in Templeton.

San Luis Obispo County Selection
From left to right: EOS Estate 1998 Paso Robles Chardonnay; Arciero 1999 California Chardonnay; EOS Estate 1998 Paso Robles Cabernet Sauvignon; Wild Horse 1999 ENZ Vineyard Lime Kiln Valley Sauvignon Blanc; Laetitia 1999 San Luis Obispo County Pinot Noir; Barnwood Vineyards 2000 Santa Barbara County Cabernet Sauvignon; Tobin James 2000 Paso Robles Charisma dessert wine; Tobin James 1998 Estate Private Stash Paso Robles Red Wine; Tobin James 1999 Cushman Vineyard Paso Robles Zinfandel.

Templeton Area Wineries

Just ten miles south of Paso Robles is Templeton, home to Ken Volk and Wild Horse Winery & Vineyards, among others. Volk is an eclectic, studying wines and vines from all over and planting dozens of varieties on his carefully mapped fifty-acre vineyard. He then meticulously blends the varietals into several interesting wines. Some are not always successful but most knowledgeable tasters accord Volk many more wins than errors, and many of his competitors respect his work enough to look to his wines for inspiration and ideas. His Pinot Noir Cheval Sauvage (French for "wild horse") is universally admired.

While Wild Horse is Templeton's largest producer, Tom Morgan takes claim for its two smallest wineries, producing just 300 cases per year each from Casa de Caballos Vineyards (where his grazing Arabian horses keep watch over the vineyards) and Santa Rita Creek Winery.

Also in Templeton, look for tiny Dover Canyon Winery, Castoro Cellars, Jan Kris Winery, Mastantuono Winery, Pesenti Winery, and one of the county's oldest, York Mountain Winery, founded in 1892.

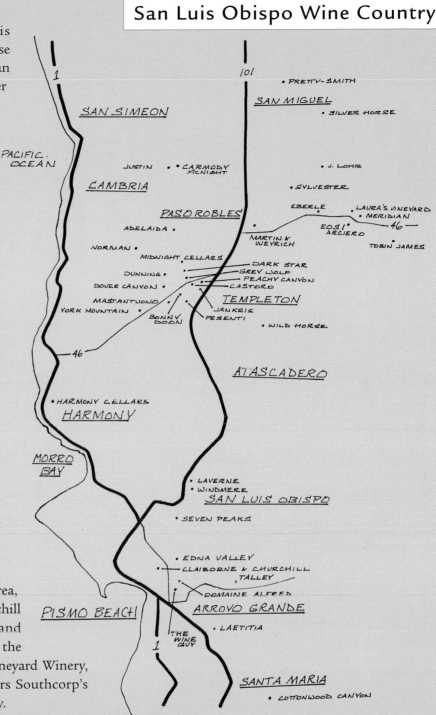

Edna Valley Wineries

In San Luis Obispo and the Edna Valley area, look for Baileyana Winery, Claiborne & Churchill Winery, Cottonwood Canyon (its winery and caves are in Santa Maria), Domaine Alfred, the 716-acre Edna Valley Vineyards, Laverne Vineyard Winery, Piedra Creek Winery, Australian winemakers Southcorp's Seven Peaks Winery, and Windemere Winery.

Continuing south, Arroyo Grande is home to the small but well-regarded Kynsi Winery and the larger and equally respected Laetitia, which produces fine Chardonnays and Pinot Noirs. Remote Saucelito Canyon Vineyards makes only 3,000 cases of a Zinfandel and has begun growing Cabernet Sauvignon grapes whereas Talley Vineyards turns out 11,000 cases including several well-reviewed Chardonnay and Pinot Noir blends.

A few other wineries throughout the county bear mention. Harmony Cellars in Harmony produces Chardonnay, Cabernet, and Pinot. Harmony is a tiny town on Highway 1 that regularly makes news itself as the entire town has been for sale for several years.

In San Miguel, another small town but with more stable ownership, look for Silver Horse Vineyards and Pretty-Smith Vineyards & Winery (formerly Mission View Winery).

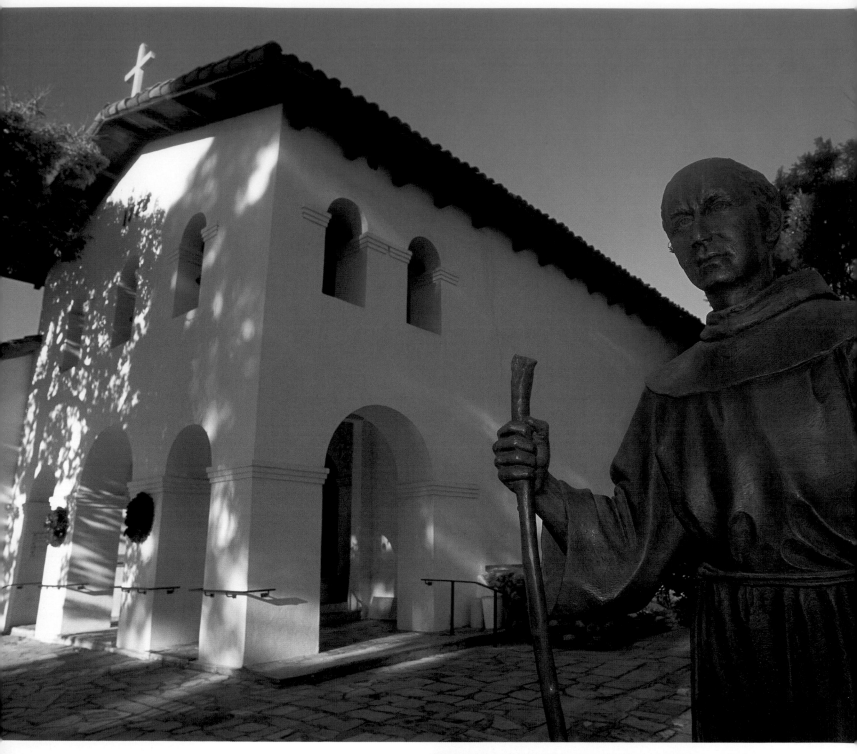

Above:
Mission San Luis Obispo de Tolosa
Padre Junipero Serra founded Mission San Luis Obispo de Tolosa in 1772.

Right:
Wine tasting in style
It is not only a stylish way to go, but a safe one. Chauffeured limousines allow wine country visitors to enjoy their experience. Every Californian winemaking region has van and limo services with chauffeurs as designated drivers.

All above:

EOS Estate Winery

EOS is the latest venture from the longtime Paso Robles winemaking Arciero family. They patterned the winery after the Benedictine monastery at Abbazia di Montecassino, Italy. The EOS name comes from Greek mythology; Eos was the goddess of the dawn and mother to the four winds, ingredients essential to the making of good wines. Paso Robles is one of San Luis Obispo County's two grape-growing regions, this one featuring hot days and comfortable nights throughout the summer months. This region produces soft, fruity reds, similar to those from the far northern end of Sonoma County's Alexander Valley.

Left and above:

Edna Valley vista

The Edna Valley is at the south end of San Luis Obispo County. Closer to the Pacific Ocean than the county's northern Paso Robles region, the Edna Valley gets ocean breezes in the afternoon and often has morning fog, more suitable to the Chardonnay grapes that make up most of the valley's vineyards.

Tobin James Cellars

The far east end of the wine tasting on Route 46 in Paso Robles offers what is perhaps the county's most enjoyable experience. Tobin James built his tasting room on the site of an old stagecoach stop and uses a mid-nineteenth century bar with its brass kick rail from Missouri. Its architectural whimsy belies Tobin James Cellars's well-regarded wines.

Right and below:

Tobin James Cellars

The summer sun heats temperatures above 105 degrees in August and September, yet nights can drop below 50 the same day throughout Paso Robles's grape-growing region. Tobin James, best known for its Zinfandels and Syrahs, raises grapes for its wines within sight of the winery. Tobin James offers its club members overnight stays in its new guest house. Each of its three sleeping rooms is furnished with plump feather beds and other luxuries.

Wild Horse Winery

At Wild Horse Winery in Templeton, harvesters peel back bird netting to retrieve the vineyard's first harvest of Blau Frankisch, a grape also known as Limberger. Owner and winemaker Ken Volk then uses whole-berry fermentation to preserve the original grape flavor in the wine.

San Luis Obispo County's Best Wines and Wineries

Eberle Zinfandels
Meridian Vineyards Cabernet
    Sauvignons
Mirassou Cabernet Sauvignons
Norman Zinfandels
Peachy Canyon Zinfandels
Talley Vineyards Chardonnays
Talley Vineyards Pinot Noirs
Tobin James Cabernet Sauvignons
Whaler Zinfandels
Wild Horse Cabernet Sauvignons

Laetitia Winery

Laetitia prepares for a fall afternoon wedding ceremony. The reception is set up in the barrel room below the tall tower. Established in 1982 as sparkling-wine producer Maison Duetz, Laetitia now concentrates nearly 90 percent of its winemaking on still varietals, including Pinot Noir and Chardonnay from its adjoining vineyards in Arroyo Grande.

San Luis Obispo County Winery and Vineyard Resources

Adelaida Cellars
5805 Adelaida Road
Paso Robles, CA 93446
805-239-8980
www.adelaida.com
Daily 11–5

Arciero Winery
5625 Highway 46 East
Paso Robles, CA 93446
805-239-2562
www.arcierowinery.com
Daily 10–5

Baileyana Winery
5880 Edna Road
San Luis Obispo, CA 93401
805-781-9463
By appointment only

Carmody McKnight Estate Wines
11240 Chimney Rock Road
Paso Robles, CA 93446
805-238-9392
www.carmodymcknight.com
Daily 10–5

Casa de Caballos Vineyards
(formerly Santa Rita Creek)
2225 Raymond Avenue
Templeton, CA 93465
805-434-1687
www.casadecaballos.com
Sat–Sun 12–5
Weekdays by appointment

Castoro Cellars
Tasting Room: 1315 North
   Bethel Road
Templeton, CA 93465
805-238-0725
888-326-3463
www.castorocellars.com
Daily 11:00–5:30

Claiborne & Churchill Winery
2649 Carpenter Canyon Road
San Luis Obispo, CA 93401
805-544-4066
www.clairbornechurchill.com
Daily 11–5

Cottonwood Canyon
4330 Sante Fe Road
San Luis Obispo, CA 93401
805-549-9463
www.cottonwoodcanyon.com
Daily 12–5:30 Memorial Day to
   Labor Day

Sat–Sun 11–5 Labor Day to
   Memorial Day
Winery and caves: 3940 Domin-
   ion Road
Santa Maria, CA 93454
805-937-9063
Daily 10:30–5:30

Courtside Cellars & Tolosa
   Winery
4910 Edna Road
San Luis Obispo, CA 93401
805-782-0300
www.tolosawinery.com
Mon–Fri 8–5

Dark Star Cellars
2985 Anderson Road
Paso Robles, CA 93446
805-237-2389
www.darkstarcellars.com
Thu–Mon 11:00–5:30

Domaine Alfred
7525 Orcutt Road
San Luis Obispo, CA 93401
805-541-9463
www.domainealfred.com
Fri–Sun 10–5

Dover Canyon Winery
4520 Vineyard Drive
Paso Robles, CA 93446
805-237-0101
www.dovercanyon.com
Fri–Sun 11–5

Dunning Vineyards
1953 Niderer Road
Paso Robles, CA 93446
805-238-4763
www.dunningvineyards.com
Fri–Sun 11–5

Eberle Winery
Highway 46
Paso Robles, CA 93446
805-238-9607
www.eberlewinery.com
Daily 10–6

Edna Valley Vineyards
2585 Biddle Ranch Road
San Luis Obispo, CA 93401
805-544-5855
www.ednavalley.com
Daily 10–5

EOS Estate Winery
5625 East Highway 46
Paso Robles, CA 93446
805-239-2562
www.eosvintage.com
Daily 11–5

Fratelli Perata Winery
1595 Arbor Road
Paso Robles, CA 93446
805-238-2809
www.fratelliperata.com
Weekends 10–5
Other times by appointment

Grey Wolf Cellars
2174 Highway 46 West
Paso Robles, CA 93446
805-237-0771
Daily 11:00–5:30

Harmony Cellars
3255 Harmony Valley Road
Harmony, CA 93455
805-927-1625
By appointment only

J. Lohr Winery
6169 Airport Road
Paso Robles, CA 93446
805-239-8900
www.jlohr.com
Daily 10–5

Jan Kris Winery
1266 Bethel Road
Templeton, CA 93465
805-434-0319
www.jankriswinery.com
Daily 11:00–5:30

Justin Vineyards & Winery
11680 Chinmmey Rock Road
Paso Robles, CA 93446
805-238-6932
www.justinwine.com
Daily 10–5

Kynsi Winery
2212 Corbett Canyon Road
Arroyo Grande, CA 93420
805-544-8461
www.kynsiwinery.com
Fri–Sun 11–5

Laetitia Winery
453 Tower Grove Drive
Arroyo Grande, CA 93420
805-481-1772
www.laetitiawine.com
www.barnwoodwine.com

Daily 11–6 Memorial Day to
   Labor Day
Daily 11–5 Labor Day to
   Memorial Day

Laura's Vineyard
5620 Highway 46 East
Paso Robles, CA 93446
805-238-6300
Daily 10–5

Laverne Vineyard Winery
3490 Sacramento Drive
San Luis Obispo, CA 93401
805-547-0616
Sat–Sun 12–4

Martin & Weyrich Winery
2610 Buena Vista Drive
Paso Robles, CA 93446
805-238-2520
www.martinweyrich.com
Daily 10–6

Mastantuono Winery
2720 Oak View Road
Templeton, CA 93465
805-238-0676
www.mastantuono.com
Daily 10–6

Meridian Vineyards
7000 Highway 46 East
Paso Robles, CA 93446
805-237-6000
www.meridianvineyards.com
Daily 10–5

Midnight Cellars
2925 Anderson Road
Paso Robles, CA 993446
805-237-9601
Daily 10:00–5:30

Norman Vineyards
7450 Vineyard Drive
Paso Robles, CA 93446
805-237-0138
www.normanvineyards.com
Daily 11–5 except major holidays

Peachy Canyon Winery
Tasting room: 1480 North Bethel
   Road
Templeton, CA 93465
805-239-1918
www.peachycanyon.com
Daily 11–5

Pesenti Winery
2900 Vineyard Drive
Templeton, CA 93465
805-434-1030
Daily 9–5

Piedra Creek Winery
6425 Mira Cielo Drive
San Luis Obipo, CA 93401
805-541-1281
By appointment only

Poalillo Wines
1888 Willow Creek Road
Paso Robles, CA 93446
805-238-0600
By appointment only

Pretty-Smith Vineyards & Winery
(formerly Mission View)
13350 North River Road
San Miguel, CA 93451
805-467-3104
www.prettysmith.com
Fri–Mon 10–5

Saucelito Canyon Vineyards
1600 Saucelito Canyon Road
Arroyo Grande, CA 93420
805-489-8762
www.saucelitocanyon.com
By appointment only

Seven Peaks Winery
5828 Orcutt Road
San Luis Obispo, CA 93401
408-781-0777
www.7peaks.com
Daily 10–5

Silver Horse Vineyards
2995 Pleasant Road
San Miguel, CA 93451
805-467-9463
www.silverhorse.com
Fri–Sun 11–5 or by appointment

Stephen Ross Wines
Available at The Wine Guy
1817 Osos Street
San Luis Obispo, CA 93401
805-546-8466
www.wineguy.net
Tues–Sat 11–7

Sylvester Winery
5115 Buena Vista Drive
Paso Robles, CA 93446
805-227-4000
www.sylvesterwinery.com
Daily 10–5

Tablas Creek Vineyard
9339 Adelaida Road
Paso Robles, CA 93446
805-237-1231
www.tablascreek.com
By appointment only

Talley Vineyards
3031 Lopez Drive
Arroyo Grande, CA 93420
805-489-0446
www.talleyvineyards.com
Daily 10:30–4:30

Tobin James Cellars
8950 Union Road
Paso Robles, CA 93446
805-239-2204
www.tobinjames.com
Daily 10–6

Vista del Rey Vineyards
7340 Drake Road
Paso Robles, CA 93446
805-467-2138
Sun 11–5 or by appointment

Wild Horse Winery & Vineyards
1437 Wild Horse Winery Court
Templeton, CA 93465
805-434-2541
www.wildhorsewinery.com
Daily 11–5

Windemere Winery
3482 Sacramento Drive, Suite E
San Luis Obispo, CA 93401
805-542-0133
www.windemerewinery.com
Daily 11:30–5:00

Windward Vineyard
1380 Live Oak Road
Paso Robles, CA 93446
805-239-2565
www.windwardvineyard.com
Fri–Sun 11–5
Mon–Thur by appointment only

York Mountain Winery
7505 York Mountain Road
Templeton, CA 93465
805-238-3925
Daily 10–5

Chapter Twelve

Santa Barbara County

The South-Central Wineries

As with other winemaking counties, there were Franciscan missions in Santa Barbara County planted with Mission grapes in the 1780s. The padres left, and the vineyards were abandoned. Then, a century later, French settlers raising sheep on Santa Cruz Island twenty-five miles off shore planted more grapes. However, it wasn't until U.C. Davis professors Maynard Amerine and A. J. Winkler examined the county's climate and soils in the early 1960s that the grape-growing potential was realized.

Santa Barbara County offers growers an affordable solution to rising land prices around the San Francisco Bay and already high costs in Napa and Sonoma. But it took time for word to spread, and in 1969, Santa Barbara County had just eleven acres planted in grape vines.

The tax loopholes of the 1970s encouraged vineyard planting and many large-scale growers rushed in, buying former cattle-ranch grazing lands and planting—as other financially shrewd and agriculturally ill-informed owners had done all over the state—the wrong grapes. Within a decade, most of those vines had been grafted over to varieties more suitable to the weather. Then more-knowledgeable winemakers began to take note. During the 1990s, Beringer, Kendall-Jackson, and Robert Mondavi all acquired large properties. By 1998, growers were raising more than 10,000 acres; at the end of 2000, the number had doubled to more than 20,000 acres.

Much of the Santa Barbara harvest goes north to winemakers in Napa and Sonoma. About half of the vines are Chardonnay, and during the 1990s, Santa Barbara Chardonnay grapes often commanded higher prices per ton than Sonoma or Napa Chardonnays.

The Santa Barbara grapes that stay within the county go to good use, however. Read any of the wine tasters and reviewers, and Santa Barbara County wines not only tell a success story but their scores reveal the results of wise, careful farming, grape growing, and winemaking.

Santa Maria Valley Wineries

As with the other counties, there are distinctive grape-growing regions in Santa Barbara. Starting in the north, just below the San Luis Obispo County line, there is the Santa Maria Valley, the coolest growing district in the county with average daytime temperature highs of just 74 degrees during its long growing season. It is in this valley that Mondavi, Beringer, and Kendall-Jackson own their largest Santa Barbara holdings and that local wineries such as Qupe Wine Cellars and Au Bon Climat have made their reputations.

Be sure to visit Byron Winery up lovely Tepusquet Canyon. The Tepusquet bridge is permanently closed so enter from farther west, along Santa Maria Mesa Road. This gives you an opportunity to see some of California's best wine grapes growing in the legendary Bien Nacido Vineyard on the north side of the road. It's a private vineyard with no winery, but in late August and September just before harvest begins, the aroma of the grapes alone is intoxicating.

Also in the Santa Maria area, don't miss Cambria Winery & Vineyard, John Kerr Wines, Foxen Vineyard, and Rancho Sisquoc Winery. The wines of small producers such as Lane Tanner can be tasted in shops in Los Olivos.

Previous page:

Santa Barbara Winery
At Pierre Lafond's experimental vineyard, grower Jeff Newton has planted Pinot Noir in four-foot-wide rows with four feet between vines. But he also has set some in six-foot-wide rows, hoping to "produce a vine that is thrifty but not stressed." These yield less fruit per vine although grapes will have more juice and hence more flavor. Still, acreage yields remain high since there are more vines planted per acre.

Santa Barbara County Selection
Left to right: Gainey 1998 Santa Ynez Valley Merlot; Gainey 1999 Santa Ynez Valley Limited Selection Sauvignon Blanc; JK Vineyards 1997 Santa Barbara County Syrah; Santa Barbara Winery 1997 Reserve Chardonnay; Babcock 1998 Mount Carmel Vineyard Chardonnay; Babcock 1999 Fathom; Byron (Mondavi) 1998 Nielson Vineyard Santa Maria Pinot Noir; Byron 1998 Sierra Madre Pinot Noir

Los Alamos Valley Wineries

The Los Alamos Valley is not as well known to many wine lovers. Its average temperatures are nearly as cool as the Santa Maria Valley, creating a great home for fine Pinot Noir grapes and desirable Chardonnays. Meridian Vineyards, owned by Napa's Beringer, and Kendall-Jackson are major growers in this valley.

While there are many good grapes in the area, there are just two wineries. Be sure to visit Bedford Thompson Winery & Vineyard and Chimere Winery's tasting room.

Santa Ynez Valley Wineries

The Santa Ynez Valley stretches more than twenty miles inland from the city of Lompoc on the west to Lake Cachuma on the east and boasts a warm growing season. While the westernmost vineyards can enjoy summer morning fog steamed off by the afternoon sun, those nearer Lake Cachuma won't see fog except in winter, and daytime highs will reach 100 degrees in July, August, and September. This valley favors Chardonnay, Sauvignon Blanc, and Riesling grapes. Growers raise reds here as well, especially Pinot Noir and Cabernet, which grow successfully in micro-climates nearer cool, foggy Lompoc.

Grape grower Jeff Newton and his partner, Larry Finkle, manage 1,200 acres of vineyards for several Santa Barbara wineries including Pierre Lafond's Santa Barbara Winery, Kathy Joseph's Fiddlehead Cellars, as well as Gainey Vineyard, Beckmen Vineyards, and Zaca Mesa Winery. They carefully match planting density to rootstock to vine type to micro-climates within each vineyard, monitoring bud-break, leaf-canopy growth, and the approach of harvest with their winemakers.

The Santa Ynez Valley, while hot for a summertime visit, makes for a wonderful day of wine tasting with good lodging available in Solvang and Buellton. Many of the wineries are located along old farm roads, as the county was largely cattle country before beef prices dropped and wine prices rose. The countryside is as appealing as the wines.

Visit Babcock Winery & Vineyards near Lompoc, and around Buellton and Solvang, look for Ballard Canyon, Buttonwood Farm Winery, Daniel Gehrs Wines, Mosby Winery, Rusack Vineyards, and especially the

Sanford Winery. Also in Solvang is the tasting room for Santa Barbara's Presidio Winery. The Hitching Post restaurant features owner Hartley Ostini's wines.

The Santa Ynez Valley opens up just west of Solvang, and one can spend an entire day tasting great wine in Los Olivos and Santa Ynez. Visit Beckmen Vineyards, Brander Vineyards, Curtis Winery, and the valley's oldest winery, Firestone Vineyard, with 540 acres founded in 1975. Don't miss the beautiful Gainey Vineyard, LinCourt Vineyards, or Richard Longoria Wines. Your tour should include Zaca Mesa Winery, Sunstone Vineyards & Winery, and Fess Parker Winery & Vineyard. Four of Santa Barbara County's finest wines—Au Bon Climat, Cold Heaven, Qupe, and Il Podere dell'Olivos (literally, "the farm of the olive trees"), a new venture by Au Bon Climat owner Jim Clendenen—are not open to the public but their wines can be tasted at the Los Olivos Tasting Room & Wine Shop. Equally interesting are the wines available at Los Olivos Vintners. Andrew Murray Vineyards's wines can be tasted at his own tasting room, also in Los Olivos.

Santa Barbara Wineries

Taking either Highway 101, following along the Gaviota Coast to Santa Barbara with the Pacific Ocean on your right, or driving California Highway 154 over San Marcos Pass with views of Santa Barbara as you descend airplane-like into the city, brings you to the last of the county's fine winemakers. In the downtown is Santa Barbara Winery, the county's oldest, founded in 1962 by architect Pierre Lafond and run by winemaker Bruce McGuire. Close by, Craig Jaffurs, who worked for McGuire for five years, has opened Jaffurs Wine Cellars. Each of these is worth a visit.

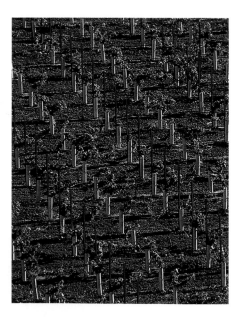

Fiddlehead Cellars
Fiddlehead expanded its Pinot Noir acreage in 2000, taking advantage of what owner and winemaker Kathy Joseph concluded were ideal conditions for the grapes, a popular and successful variety in the county. Western Santa Barbara County vineyards benefit from the Pacific Ocean's cool breezes and fog to modulate the sun's heat.

The Celebration of Harvest
Santa Barbara–area chefs provide food for The Celebration of Harvest. This annual tasting benefit is also a celebration. Normally, the majority of the vineyards are already harvested, and so the sleepless nights that characterize grape picking are replaced with weekend and evening promotional events.

Gainey Vineyard

Santa Barbara County is divided into four appellations, including Santa Barbara, on the ocean side of the Santa Ynez Mountains, Santa Ynez Valley on the inland side, Santa Maria at the north end of the county, and the most recent designation, Santa Rita Hills, at the west end encompassing the Lompoc and Buellton areas. Grape growing is perhaps Santa Barbara County's fastest growing industry with 9,000 acres planted in 1996 and more than 18,000 by the end of 2000.

Santa Barbara County Winery and Vineyard Resources

Los Alamos Valley

Bedford Thompson Winery &
    Vineyard
9303 Alisos Canyon Road
Los Alamos, CA 93440
805-344-2107
www.bedfordthompsonwinery.com
Daily 10–5

Carrari Vineyards
P.O. Box 556
Los Alamos, CA 93440
805-344-4000
By appointment only

Santa Maria Valley

Au Bon Climat
Qupe Wine Cellars
Cold Heaven
Il Podere dell'Olivos
Santa Maria, CA 93454
805-937-9801
www.aubonclimat.com
Not open to the public
Tasting at Los Olivos Tasting
    Room & Wine Shop

Byron Winery
5230 Tepusquet Road
Santa Maria, CA 93454
805-937-7288
www.byronwines.com
Daily 10–5 April–October
Daily 10–4 November–March

Cambria Winery & Vineyards
5475 Chardonnay Lane
Santa Maria, CA 93454
805-937-8091
www.cambriawines.com
Sat–Sun 10–5
Weekdays by appointment

Chimere Winery
Tasting room: 425 Bell Street
Los Alamos, CA
805-344-9907
Fri–Mon 11–5

Cottonwood Canyon Vineyard &
    Winery
3940 Dominion Road
Santa Maria, CA 93454
805-937-9063
www.cottonwoodcanyon.com
Daily 10:30–5:30

Foxen Vineyard
7200 Foxen Canyon Road
Santa Maria, CA 93454
805-937-4251
Fri–Mon 12–4

John Kerr Wines
900 East Stowell Road
Santa Maria, CA 93456
805-688-5337
By appointment only

Lane Tanner Winery
Box 286
Santa Maria, CA 93456
805-929-1826
Not open to public
Tasting at Los Olivos Tasting
    Room & Wine Shop

Rancho Sisquoc
6600 Foxen Canyon Road
Santa Maria, CA 93454
805-934-4332
www.ranchosisquoc.com
Daily 10–4

Santa Ynez Valley

Andrew Murray Vineyards
6701 Foxen Canyon Road
Los Olivos, CA 93441
805-686-9604
www.andrewmurrayvineyards.com
Sat–Sun. 11–4 or by appoint-
    ment
Tasting room: 2901 Grand
    Avenue Suite A
Los Olivos, CA 93441
805-693-9644
Daily 11:00–5:30

Babcock Winery & Vineyard
5175 East Highway 246
Lompoc, CA 93436
805-736-1455
www.babcockwinery.com
Fri–Sun 10:30–4:00 or by
    appointment

Ballard Canyon
1825 Ballard Canyon Road
Solvang, CA 93463
805-688-7585
By appointment only

Beckmen Vineyards
2670 Ontiveros Road
Los Olivos, CA 93441
805-688-8664
Daily 11–5 June–August
Fri–Sun 11–5 September–May

Brander Vineyards
Highway 154 at Roblar Avenue
Los Olivos, CA 93441
805-688-2455
www.brander.com
Daily 11–4 October–April
Daily 11–5 May–September

Buttonwood Farm Winery
1500 Alamo Pintado Road
Solvang, CA 93463
805-688-3032
www.buttonwoodwinery.com
Daily 11–5

Curtis Winery
5249 Foxen Canyon Road
Los Olivos, CA 93441
805-686-8999
www.curtiswinery.com
Daily 11–6 Memorial Day to
    Labor Day
Daily 10–5 Labor Day to
    Memorial Day

Daniel Gehrs Wines
2939 Grand Avenue
Los Olivos, CA 93441
805-686-1229
www.dgwines.com
Daily 11–6

Fess Parker Winery
6200 Foxen Canyon Road
Los Olivos, CA 93441
805-688-1545
www.fessparker.com
Daily 10–5

Fiddlehead Cellars
Office: 606 Pena Drive, Suite 500
Davis, CA 95616
530-756-4550
Tasting at Los Olivos Tasting
    Room & Wine Shop

Firestone Vineyard
5017 Zaca Station Road
Los Olivos, CA 93441
805-688-3940
www.firestonevineyard.com
Daily 10–5

Gainey Vineyard
3950 East Highway 246
Santa Ynez, CA 93460
805-688-0558
www.gaineyvineyard.com
Daily 10–5

Hitching Post Restaurant &
    Hartley Ostini Wines Tasting
    Room
406 East Highway 246
Buellton, CA 93427
805-688-0676
www.hitchingpost2.com
Daily 4:00–9:30

Kalyra
P.O. Box 865
Buellton, CA 93427
805-963-0274
By appointment only

LinCourt Vineyards
343 North Refugio Road
Santa Ynez, CA 93460
805-688-8381
Daily 10–5

Mosby Winery
9496 Santa Rosa Road
Buellton, CA 93427
805-688-2415
www.mosbywines.com
Mon–Fri 10–4
Sat–Sun 10–5

Richard Longoria Wines
2935 Grand Avenue
Los Olivos, CA 93441
805-688-0305
www.longoriawine.com
Mon, Wed–Thur 12:00–4:30
Fri–Sun 11:00–4:30

Rusack Vineyards
1819 Ballard Canyon Road
Solvang, CA 93463
805-688-1278
www.rusackvineyards.com
Daily 11–5

Sanford Winery
7250 Santa Rosa Road
Buellton, CA 93427
805-688-3300
Daily 11–4

Stolpman Vineyards
4120 Lorraine Road
Rancho Palos Verdes, CA 90275
562-435-8300

Sunstone Vineyards & Winery
125 Refugio Road
Santa Ynez, CA 93460
805-688-9463
www.sunstonewinery.com
Daily 10–4

Zaca Mesa Winery
6905 Foxen Canyon Road
Los Olivos, CA 93441
805-688-9339
www.zacamesa.com
Daily 10–4

Santa Barbara County

Jaffurs Wine Cellars
819 East Montecito Street
Santa Barbara, CA 93103
805-962-7003
www.jaffurswine.com
By appointment only

Presidio Winery
805-740-9463
www.presidiowinery.com
Tasting at Wine Country
1539 Mission Drive #C
Solvang, CA 93463
805-686-9699
www.winecountrytoo.com
Sun–Thur 8:30–5
Fri–Sat 8:30–7

Santa Barbara Winery
202 Anacapa Street
Santa Barbara, CA 93101
805-963-3633
www.sbwinery.com
Daily 10–5

Tasting Rooms and Other Information

Santa Barbara County contains a number of small winemakers who rely on either of two area retail outlets to serve as their tasting rooms:

Los Olivos Tasting Room & Wine Shop
2905 Grand Avenue
Los Olivos, CA 93441
805-688-7406
www.losolivoswines.com
Daily 11:00–5:30

Los Olivos Wine & Spirits Emporium
2531 Grand Avenue
Los Olivos, CA 93441
805-688-4409
www.sbwines.com
Daily 11–6

Santa Barbara Vinters' Association
P.O. Box 1558
Santa Ynez, CA 93460
800-218-0881
Maps and information

Santa Barbara County's Best Wines and Wineries

Au Bon Climat Barberas
Au Bon Climat Bien Nacido Chardonnays
Au Bon Climat Chardonnays
Babcock Chardonnays
Babcock Sauvignon Blancs
Brander Bouchet Proprietary Red Wines
Buttonwood Farm Merlots
Buttonwood Farm Sauvignon Blancs
Byron Estate and Reserve Chardonnays
Byron Sauvignon Blancs
Calambria Chardonnays
Fess Parker Chardonnays
Firestone Cabernet Sauvignons
Firestone Merlots
Foxen Chardonnays
Gainey Limited Selection Cabernet Franc
Gainey Limited Selection Sauvignon Blanc
Gainey Merlots
Il Podere dell'Olivos Barberas
Kendall-Jackson's JSJ Signature Series Chardonnays

Longoria Chardonnays
Rancho Sisquoc Sauvignon Blancs
Sanford Chardonnays
Sanford Sauvignon Blancs
Santa Barbara Winery Cabernet Sauvignons
Steele Goodchild Chardonnays

Gainey Vineyard

In the Santa Ynez Valley, growers and winemakers such as Gainey, with eighty-four acres of vines surrounding its winery, gather the rest of its grapes from its forty-acre vineyard much further west in the county. Opened in 1984, Gainey has been described by writers from the *Los Angeles Times* as "one of the most beautiful wineries in the world" and by *Wine Spectator* as "one of the best wineries to visit on California's Central Coast." The winery hosts cooking classes, outdoor concerts, evening story-telling programs, and its annual harvest "crush party" in the winery or on vineyard grounds.

Chapter Thirteen

Southern California

Wines of the South

Grilled Portobello
Mushroom

Los Angeles County Wineries

While California winemaking first flourished in the Los Angeles area, only one winery, San Antonio, still survives—and thrives—near downtown. With city real estate trading hands at millions of dollars an acre, the Riboli family that owns San Antonio raises their grapes on 600 acres of vineyards they own in Monterey, in Napa's Rutherford, in Sonoma's Alexander Valley, and near Paso Robles, where their red-wine making facility is located.

"We strive for ultimate fruit character in every step from the vine to the bottle," says Steve Riboli, grandnephew of San Antonio founder Santa Cambianica. "We can't cover up any mistakes, so we try not to make any mistakes." San Antonio now produces eleven varietals in five brands, comprising three Chardonnays, three Cabernets, two Pinots, a Sirah, a Pinot Gris, and a Muscat Canelli. A Los Angeles Cultural Historical Landmark, San Antonio's visitor tour shows a photographic history of early Los Angeles city agriculture—Jean-Louis Vignes's first vineyards were less than a mile away—as well as their white-wine making facilities. In addition to an extraordinary wine shop selling not only San Antonio's products but also a fine assortment of the competition, the winery also houses the busy Maddalena Restaurant. Open daily for lunch, it offers ten seasonal food specialties prepared while you wait.

Remarkably there are a few other boutique wineries in Los Angeles County, some who buy grapes elsewhere, such as Donatoni in Inglewood, but at least two others grow their own. Tom Jones, the former chairman of aviation giant Northrop, has found a suitable eight-acre micro-climate in Bel-Air near Beverly Hills and raises Cabernet Sauvignon, Merlot, and Cabernet Franc. He produces just 500 cases a year of his highly regarded Moraga Vineyards blended Cab.

In Malibu's Newton Canyon, George Rosenthal grows twenty-four acres of Cabernet, Chardonnay, and Merlot. Rosenthal's Malibu Hills Vineyard now produces 5,000 cases a year, and offers tastings and tours by appointment.

San Bernardino County Wineries

At one time, growers raised more than 37,000 acres of grapes throughout Southern California, some 6,000 of them belonging to Secondo Guasti near Cucamonga in San Bernardino County. The three P's—Phylloxera, Pierce's disease, and Prohibition—decimated Guasti and others.

Today only winemaker Joseph Filippi remains, with just 400 acres scattered through an area of light and heavy industry. Driving around Cucamonga in the summer and early fall, keep your eyes open. In large open plots of seemingly abandoned land, you can see hundreds of old growth, deep-rooted Zinfandel and Grenache vines poking their deep green leaves above the surrounding dried grasses. Most of the rest of Filippi's grapes come from Monterey and Napa.

Orange County Wineries

In Orange County, where there were once thousands of acres of wine grapes, there are now just two acres. Robert Mondavi has a small demonstration vineyard—just twenty-one densely planted short rows of Johannisberg Riesling grapes—at his Golden Vine Winery on an acre inside Disney's California Adventure theme park.

Ever the educator, Mondavi introduces park visitors to winemaking in his Barrel Room theater with a video called "Seasons of the Vine." Adjacent to the vineyard and theater is a gift shop, deli, and wine bar selling wine by the glass, one of the few places within Disneyland where wine is available. Above these are two restaurants, the Vineyard Room and The Terrace.

In Newport Beach, Richard Moriarity harvested his first grapes in August 2001. His 700-vine, one-acre Newport Beach Vineyard & Winery grows Cabernet Sauvignon, Merlot, Cabernet Franc, Petit Verdot, and Malbec on a three-and-a-half-acre plot near Irvine Avenue and University Drive. He expects production to begin at seventy cases a year.

Riverside County Wineries

It's not until you get farther south and east in Southern California that grape growing and winemaking reappears on a larger scale. In sunny Temecula in Riverside County, a dozen or more vineyards and wineries have opened in the past quarter century, spurred by the Rancho California development that set aside 90,000 acres for housing, commercial uses, farming, and a large man-made lake.

While the region can be hot during the summer days, the wineries are open year round, and it's a pleasant and easy drive from San Diego to spend a day wine tasting and dining. *Temecula* is a Pala Indian word meaning "where the sun shines through the mist," and the region's vineyards thrive because of the cool air sucked through Rainbow Gap between the Santa Margarita Mountains and the Merriam Mountains.

In 1969, Eli Callaway was among the first to sense the potential for growing primarily Chardonnay grapes and secondarily, Sauvignon and Riesling. (Other growers have begun planting Cabernet and Syrah grapes with promising results.) Sadly, Callaway's vineyards were ravaged by Pierce's disease in 2000. While the vineyards look sparse—they're not replanting until the disease is finally controlled—Callaway owners Allied Domecq make it clear it intends to stay in Temecula and plans to increase production to nearly 600,000 cases of Callaway Coastal wines a year.

All above:
Callaway Vineyards & Winery
With a goal of 600,000 cases a year, Callaway has been taking in a huge supply of new American- and French-oak barrels to age its grapes. The winery and tasting room will stay right where they are in Temecula even as its grapes travel miles farther. Callaway owner Allied Domecq remains committed to southern California. Visitors to Callaway may taste its recently bottled Callaway Coastal vintages.

Mount Palomar Winery in Temecula hosts a candlelight barrel-room tasting in December in which some sixty invited guests and good customers sample the delicacies of a local restaurant served with five different Mount Palomar releases. During the evening, owner Peter Poole and winemaker Etienne Cowper describe for their guests what the wine is, how it was made, and how it fits with the food served. Guests walk past barrels and fermentation tanks, threading their way through the winery, eating and tasting as they learn more about wine in general and Mount Palomar's offerings in particular.

Be sure also to visit Hart Winery, Cilurzo Vineyard & Winery, and Thornton Winery, primarily for its sparkling wines. Thorton also is home to the Cafe Champagne restaurant. In warmer weather, patrons can enjoy lunch or dinner on a covered, shaded terrace and or more elegant dining inside year round.

Also visit Van Roekel Vineyard & Winery, Falkner Winery (formerly Temecula Crest), Santa Margarita Winery, Keyways Winery & Vineyard, Miramonte Winery & Celebration Cellars, Filsinger Winery, Maurice Car'rie Winery, Baily Winery, and Stuart Cellars.

J. Filippi Winery
Almost defying credulity, these eighty-year-old Grenache vines have survived drought, Prohibition, the rise of heavy industry in the suburbs, and changing public wine tastes. Yet they still produce grapes for J. Filippi in Rancho Cucamonga in San Bernardino County. These vines use their extremely deep taproots to pull up moisture from the water table far below the unirrigated surface.

Mount Palomar Winery
Mount Palomar Winery in Temecula celebrates the winter holidays with an annual early December Candlelight Barrel Room Tasting. Winemaker Etienne Cowper and winery President Peter Poole, who pours for one of his guests, serve seven of their wines to accompany seven courses of food from a local caterer.

Thornton Winery

Thornton produced sparkling wines when it first opened in 1981 and developed a strong reputation. However since 1993, Thornton has added still varietals to its list and continues to gather awards and loyal followers. Many also know Thornton for its evening jazz performances, among the best live entertainment in Riverside County. Thornton is another winery that emphasizes fine food with its fine wines. Luncheon and dinner guests enjoy the benefits of fresh herbs grown in their garden just a few yards away from the gourmet kitchen of Thornton's Café Champagne restaurant. Thornton produces about 18,000 cases a year, of which about half are sparkling blends.

Southern California's Best Wines and Wineries

Callaway Coastal
Leeward Vineyards Cabernet Sauvignons
Ojai Pisoni Vineyard Pinot Noirs
Ojai Syrahs

Golden Vine Winery

At Disneyland's California Adventure, visitors stroll past Robert Mondavi's Golden Vine Winery with its twenty-one rows of densely planted Riesling vines. It is an ironic return to history: In 1859, the first settlers moved onto twenty-acre homesteads to raise wine grapes. At the Golden Vine Winery, a number of displays and exhibits help California Adventure visitors understand the aromas and flavors as well as the art and science of wine and winemaking. Just as at Disneyland, the California Adventure features an afternoon parade along its main pathway. Visitors line the walkway in front of the Golden Vine vineyard and winery. The Mondavi facility includes a Barrel Room theater explaining how wine is made, a gift shop and deli, and a gourmet restaurant overlooking the park.

Southern California Winery and Vineyard Resources

Los Angeles County

Donatoni Winery
10604 South La Cienega
    Boulevard
Inglewood, CA 90304
310-645-5445
By appointment only

Moraga Vineyards
650 Sepulveda Boulevard
Los Angeles, CA 90031
310-471-8560
Not open to public

Rosenthal Wines
Malibu Canyon Vineyard
1-800-814-0733
www.rosenthalestatewines.com
By appointment only

San Antonio Winery
737 Lamar Street
Los Angeles, CA 90031
323-223-1401
www.sanantoniowinery.com
Daily 10–6
Maddalena Restaurant
Daily 11–5

Orange County

Golden Vine Winery
Disney's California Adventure
1313 South Harbor Boulevard
Anaheim, CA 92803
714-327-8050
www.robertmondavi.com
Disneyland Park hours
1-877-700-3476

Riverside County

Baily Winery
33440 La Serena Way
Temecula, CA 92591
909-676-9463
www.baily.com
Daily 10–5

Callaway Winery
32720 Rancho California Road
Temecula, CA 92589
909-676-4001
www.callawaycoastal.com
Daily 10:30–4:45

Cilurzo Winery
41220 Calle Contento
Temecula, CA 92592
909-676-5250
www.cilurzowine.com
Daily 10–5

Falkner Winery
(formerly Temecula Crest
    Winery)
40620 Calle Contento
Temecula, CA 92592
909-676-8231
www.falknerwinery.com
Daily 10–5

Filsinger Winery
39050 De Portola Road
Temecula, CA 92592
909-302-6363
www.filsinger-winery.com
Fri 11:00–4:30
Sat–Sun 10–5

Hart Winery
41300 Avenida Biona
Temecula, CA 92591
909-676-6300
Sat–Sun 9:00–4:30

Keyways Winery & Vineyard
37338 De Portola Road
Temecula, CA 92592
909-302-7888
www.keywayswinery.com
Daily 10–5

Maurice Car'rie Winery
34225 Rancho California Road
Temecula, Ca 92592
909-676-1711
www.winesplus.com
Daily 10–5

Miramonte Winery & Celebration Cellars
33410 Rancho California Road
Temecula, CA 92591
909-506-5500
www.miramontewinery.com
Daily 10–5

Mount Palomar Winery
33820 Rancho California Road
Temecula, CA 92591
909-676-5047
www.mountpalomar.com
Daily 10:00–4:45

Santa Margarita Winery
33490 Madera de Playa
Temecula, CA 92592
909-676-4431
Weekends 11:00–4:30 from
    November until sold out

Stuart Cellars
33515 Rancho California Road
Temecula, CA 92591
909-646-6414
www.stuartcellars.com
Daily 10–5

Temecula Wine-Growers
    Association
34567 Rancho California Road
Temecula, CA 92591
909-699-6586
www.temeculawines.org

Thornton Winery
32575 Rancho California Road
Temecula, CA 92591
909-699-0099
www.thorntonwine.com
Daily 10–5
Café Champagne restaurant
Lunch: 11–4, dinner: 5–9 Tues–
    Sun

Van Roekel Vineyard & Winery
34567 Rancho California Road
Temecula, CA 92592
909-699-6961
Daily 10–5

San Bernardino County

J. Filippi Winery
12467 Base Line Road
Rancho Cucamongo, CA 91739
909-899-5755
www.josephfilippiwinery.com
Daily 10–6

Ventura County

Leeward Winery
2784 Johnson Drive
Ventura, CA 93001
805-656-5054
Daily 10–4

Ojai Winery
P.O. Box 952
Oak View, CA 93022
805-649-1674
www.ojaivineyard.com
Not open to the public

Old Creek Ranch Winery
10024 East Old Creek Road
Ojai, CA 93023
805-649-4132
www.oldcreekranchwinery.com
Sat–Sun 11–5
Weekdays by appointment

Index

About the Author

Writer and photographer Randy Leffingwell lives in Ojai, California, although he was raised in the Chicago suburbs. He received a Bachelor of Science in Journalism from Kansas University in 1970. He worked two years for the Kansas City *Times* before joining the Chicago *Sun-Times*. He remained there for nine years, then worked for one year as Associate Editor at *AutoWeek* magazine in Detroit. In 1984, he joined the staff of the Los Angeles *Times* as writer/photographer. While at the *Times*, he began writing and photographing non-fiction books on Americana, covering subjects as diverse as barns in America and Harley-Davidsons. He left the *Times* in 1995 to work on books full time. Among his other books is *Lighthouses of the Pacific Coast*, also published by Voyageur Press.

Acknowledgments

To everyone who made introductions and phone calls, and who opened winery doors and vineyard fences to me, I am most deeply grateful. In particular, I wish to thank: Brian Babcock of Babcock Winery & Vineyard; Ted Bennett, Deborah Cahn, and Jim Klein of Navarro Vineyards; Jody Bogle of Bogle Winery; Nan Campbell of Carneros Quality Alliance; Mike Carhardt of Vogelzang Winery; Rachel Chacon of Stag's Leap Wine Cellars; Michael Charles of Elliston Vineyards; Jerry Clark of Clark Custom Harvesting; Etienne Cowper, Peter Poole, Martine Gallegos, and Denise Sutterfield of Mount Palomar Winery; Stephen Dale, Iris Reyes, and Susan Lewis Scarbrough of Buena Vista Carneros; Melissa and Joseph Damiano of Smith Vineyard & Winery; Jim Frediani of Frediani Vineyards; Allan Green of Greenwood Ridge Vineyards; Stephanie Grubbs of Sebastiani Vineyards; Dorothy and Cheryl Indelicato of Delicato Family Winery; Bud Bradley of Clay Station Vineyards; Bill Petrovik of San Bernabe Vineyards; Tom Jordan, Lisbeth Holmefjord, Rob Davis, and Sara Quider of Jordan Vineyard & Winery; Kathy Joseph of Fiddlehead Cellars; John Livingston, Diane Livingston, and Trent Moffett of Livingston Moffett Winery; Carole Loomis of Bouchaine Winery; John, Barbara, and Michelle MacCready of Sierra Vista Winery & Vineyards; Scott McLeod, Shannon Carstens, and Kathleen Talbert of Niebaum-Coppola Estate Winery; Ira Metheny of Metheny Builders; Peter Mondavi Sr. and Peter Mondavi Jr., Denise Breese, Jack Colaiaco, and Ron Rosenbrand of Charles Krug Winery; Jeff Newton and Larry Finkle of Coastal Vineyard Management; Russ and Sally Nyborg of Whaler Vineyard; Eliud Ortiz of Galante Vineyards; Sally Ottoson of Pacific Star Winery; Ed Raetz of U.C. Riverside; Karen Rew of Grapevine Wreath Co.; Steve Riboli and David Vergari of San Antonio Winery; Nancy Sean of Callaway Winery; Rudy and Dorothy Smith of Mount St. Helena Vineyards; Leon Sobon of Shenandoah Vineyards & Sobon Estate; Fred and Sally Schweiger of Schweiger Vineyard; Alex Vaernewyck, Andrew Byars, Ramiro Herrara, and Douglas Rennie of Seguin Moreau Tonnellerie; Ken Volk, Karl Wicka, and Matt Garretson of Wild Horse Winery & Vineyards; Edward and Debbie Wallo of Yorkville Cellars; and Christine Wente of Wente Vineyards.

In addition, I am most grateful to my friend and editor Michael Dregni, who proposed and then supervised this project. He patiently extended deadlines because I was simply having too much fun to let this book go.

And finally, thanks to my friend Casey Barr for his valuable assistance in photographing the regional wine bottles.